T0265894

BEYOND
Good and Evil

BEYOND
Good and Evil
A Life in Boxing

GLYN RHODES MBE

WITH MARK TURLEY

First published by Pitch Publishing, 2022

Pitch Publishing
9 Donnington Park,
85 Birdham Road,
Chichester,
West Sussex,
PO20 7AJ
www.pitchpublishing.co.uk
info@pitchpublishing.co.uk

A CIP catalogue record is available for this book
from the British Library.

ISBN 978 1 80150 375 4

Typesetting and origination by Pitch Publishing

Printed and bound in Great Britain by TJ Books, Padstow

Contents

This book is dedicated to all the boxing teachers and coaches who spend hours in gyms up and down the country 24/7, teaching kids how to become better people. Most of these coaches never get any recognition for the work they do week after week, month after month, year after year. Never mind the big-money champions, they are the true heroes of our sport.

It's also dedicated to all those going through difficult times within themselves. My advice is to find someone to speak to.

This book is also dedicated to the memory of Scott Westgarth, RIP.

Acknowledgements

I NEED to thank my grandparents, Joe and Annie, for my start. My parents, Wendy and Freddie, for everything. Dave Davies, for encouraging me to promote my first amateur and professional show. I couldn't have done it without his encouragement. Herol 'Bomber' Graham, who I met at 16 and enabled me to do so much as a trainer. Brian Anderson, who always stopped me killing someone in the gym. My childhood friend, Darren Wright, who helped me in the beginning. And Brendan Ingle, because who knows where I'd be, had I not met him. On top of this, I'd like to thank anybody else I've forgotten who ever helped me. Also, the people who didn't help me, but made me the person I am today.

A big thank you to my kids because it seems that over the years, I've spent more time with other people's kids than I did my own. That wasn't a conscious choice. It was just the way things turned out.

Glyn Rhodes, June 2022

Preface from co-author, Mark Turley

BOXING, EH?

I've tried to focus on other subjects. The world is full of fascinating things to write about, or so I believe, but boxing always pulls me back. I leave it for a year or two, then it's there again. People often say I must love the sport to keep returning to it. That's too much of an easy line, though.

In many ways, I'm deeply troubled by it. Its hullabaloo and nonsense, its greed, the casual violence which surrounds it, the damage it causes, which can be immediate and life-threatening, or slow, sinister and creeping – all of these things sit uneasily with me. Yet boxing also has a rawness which won't let me go.

I think it's because so much in the modern world feels incredibly artificial, but not what happens in a boxing ring. No matter what's been said beforehand, whatever you are gets exposed in there. Brave, afraid, reckless, self-doubting, heroic, ready, focused, old, tired – it doesn't matter,. Whatever is inside you will show.

It's all truth once the bell goes.

The other thing that keeps bouncing back at me is Sheffield. The steel city has a great fighting tradition and a fair shout to call itself Britain's boxing capital, but I'm a Londoner and have no historical connection to South Yorkshire, at all. The wind's baltic and all the hills do my knees in. Despite that, I seem to keep ending up there.

I first met Glyn Rhodes MBE at a book launch in Sheffield in 2015. The boxer I was working with, Jerome Wilson, was not his fighter. In fact, Glyn had managed and trained his last opponent. Despite that, he was one of the first to arrive at the event and one of the last to leave. We spoke about his life and career. He mentioned then that he wanted to do a book one day. I was intrigued.

Over the coming years, as I came to Sheffield again and again, Glyn's name kept cropping up. Whether it was in connection to high-level professional boxing, title fights and trips abroad, or the junior classes he holds at his Sheffield Boxing Centre gym, he was always spoken of fondly. Not that he's an angel, of course. There aren't any of those in boxing, but he obviously exerted a positive influence over Sheffield and therefore British boxing for several decades.

When we spoke on the phone last year and he said he was ready to tell his story, I knew immediately it was one I should do. Glyn's experiences during 40-odd years in the fight game, from the positive, to the euphoric to the tragic, have the scope to encapsulate all there is about this most primal of sports.

So, I won't fall into the trap of saying this is my last boxing book. I've said that before, but I believe this will be the one that sums the whole thing up.

Remember, it's all truth once the bell goes.

Ding, ding.

Introduction – 'the air was full of feathers'

THE SHRINK sits neatly, legs crossed at the knee, very composed and self-contained, straight-backed on her chair. I imagine she does yoga in her spare time, eats vegan food, rides a bicycle. She looks at me softly, as if there's no pressure. Not what I was expecting, at all. You know the cliché. Sterile, white rooms, stern faces and questions like, 'So, tell me about your mother.'

She's not bad looking, this one – brown hair, hazel eyes, late thirties. I'm not sure if that helps or not, but I knew, for sure, that I wanted a woman. A male psychiatrist would have been awkward. I'm not opening myself up to a fella.

Her office, if that's the right word for it, looks like a lounge, in a big old manor house near the centre of town. There's a couple of easy chairs and a sofa. I sit down, then put my hat and keys on the coffee table beside me. She smiles nicely.

'Good morning,' she says.

'Morning.' I don't like the way my voice sounds, thin, a bit nervy. 'This err …' The words stick in my throat.

'Go on,' she encourages me.

'This in't something I thought I'd ever do.'

'I know,' she says.

What she doesn't know is that I've been struggling badly for a few years. Life's been like swimming through treacle. Boxing can get you like that. The doctor prescribed anti-depressants, but I couldn't bring myself to take them.

I had always dismissed this stuff. If someone in the gym said they were depressed, I would have told them to do some press-ups, go for a run, pull themselves together. It's different when it happens to you, though, isn't it?

But in my mind, I'm not depressed. It's a deeper issue, one that curdled inside me until it turned rotten. One day, I confided in my right-hand man at the gym.

'I reckon you should go and see a psychiatrist,' he said.

'What?' I narrowed my eyes.

'I've been to see a psychiatrist,' he went on, as if it was the most normal thing in the world. This was a guy who had chalked up 27 professional fights and led a right life outside the ring. A man's man. As an inmate, he had been involved in the Strangeways prison riots in 1990. He'd been in the Foreign Legion, done all sorts, but here he was telling me how a shrink helped him get over his internalised trauma.

'Thanks,' I said. 'I'll think about that.'

I still took my time, though, turning it over and over, often in the middle of the night. That can got kicked down the road for two years. Then, at last, I looked through the Yellow Pages and found her number. A few days after that, I even plucked up the courage to call. It went straight to voicemail, so I hung up. What do you say to a psychiatrist's answerphone?

'Good morning. My name's Glyn and I think I'm cracking up.'

I did the exact same thing three times. After the last one, she must have seen my number appearing repeatedly and called me back. Boy, was that an embarrassing conversation.

Now here I am.

She begins talking, nice enough, just chit-chat really, but all the time, I'm on edge. I'm waiting for the questions to start, the real questions, the ones that will get me to talk about the scenes in my memory.

She asks about my childhood, about what made me happy, what I used to enjoy. Very slowly I feel myself start to unravel, as if she's a cat and I'm a ball of string. Before I know it, I'm just talking, wittering on about my mum and grandad, Brendan Ingle, my ex-wife, my kids, pretty much everything.

Near the end of our allotted time, she asks if I want to talk about it. Just like that. She's relaxed me by then and catches me on the back foot. Crafty. The punches that get through are always the ones you don't see.

'Err … the air,' I say.

She looks a bit puzzled, shakes her head slightly.

'The air?'

It is so hard to say it. I have to cough it out.

'The air was full of fucking feathers.'

Immediately I know it's too much for me, but there's no way I am going to cry in front of her, so I scowl, snatch up my hat and keys, then storm out. The door slams as I go.

Out on the street, before I get in my car, I look back at the house and think of her inside, reflecting, going through her notes, analysing my behaviour.

I know that soon, I'm going to have to go back.

1

A LOT of boxing people have messy childhoods. You know the story, right? The kid from the wrong side of the tracks, saved from the streets by the gym. Boxing as an escape route, channelling inner rage, fighting the demons.

I don't think I'm one of those. Not really. I do sometimes wonder what made me a fighter but have not come up with a solid answer. I often feel like I just fell into it.

I never knew my dad. Perhaps we can pin it on that?

My mum, Wendy, was just 18 when I was born in 1959, and I was brought up in her parents' house in the Attercliffe area of north-east Sheffield. Later on, we moved to Firth Park, also in the north of the city. I was aware from a young age that I did not have two normal parents like other kids. But my grandparents more than made up for that.

Joe, my grandad, was a typical man of his generation. No nonsense, no sentiment, always working, always fixing things in the house. On one occasion, when I was still in nappies, all his tools were laid on the floor, and I picked up a big clawhammer, raised it and tried to swing it, as I had seen him do. The thing was so heavy it took both my hands to lift it, and once I got it up at arms' length, it could only do one thing – come back down – which it did, on top of my head.

So, I was about two years old when I both dealt and suffered my first knockout. Glyn Rhodes done in by Glyn Rhodes. Perhaps that was a sign of the future.

Like most Sheffield men in the 60s, Grandad worked in the steel industry. To me, with his big, muscular arms and Brylcreemed hair, he was a hero. He had fought in World War Two, and actually took part in the D-Day landings in Normandy. Like most ex-soldiers, he had boxed a bit too, but Grandad was a reserved man and didn't speak much about his experiences.

My grandmother, Annie, was more talkative and provided a soothing, dependable presence. That was important, because when I was at primary school, my mother met and started dating a new man called Freddie. Of course, this was perfectly normal. After all, she was still a young woman with her whole life ahead of her, but I struggled with the change and gave everyone a hard time. I guess it was tough for me to accept that after all those years I was now expected to share her.

I started playing up, probably just a vain attempt to regain Mum's attention, to make her all mine again. I became moody and stroppy.

One summer evening during that difficult time, I was messing around on the road with some other kids when a grown man, who obviously I had annoyed somehow, pushed me off my bike. He gave me a little slap, and I ran off crying, back to the house. My gran asked me what was wrong.

'Some–fella–slapped–me,' I said, through staccato sobs.

Immediately, she woke Grandad, who had fallen asleep in his chair after work, as was his habit. I was still crying.

'Stop blubbin' and talk to me!' he said, grabbing me by the shoulders.

I explained.

'Right,' he said, rising from his chair, heading for the door. 'We'll sort that out then.'

Gran grabbed me by the arm and dragged me out after him. As we followed him out on to the road, Grandad rolled up his sleeves.

The man and my bike were both still in the street as Grandad strode out in the early evening light. It was like a dream. He calmly walked up to the guy, as if it was the most natural thing in the world, said something I couldn't hear, then cracked him on the chin with a right hook.

The guy went down hard, like a puppet whose strings had been cut. Grandad turned to me, with a curious light in his eyes. 'Get your bike, Glyn,' he said. 'It's nearly bedtime.'

'Yes, Grandad.'

Everything seemed different right then. The street shone. Grandad was suddenly about ten feet tall. The only time I had seen anything like that was in movies.

That punch stayed with me for ages. I must have relived it a thousand times. It was such a simple action, yet had such huge effects, on the man who had thrown it as much as the man who received it. God, how I loved my grandfather. I thought he was Superman.

Not long after that, I was in bed one night and heard shouting downstairs. The voices were instantly familiar. Mum and Grandad were arguing.

I crept down and it was clear what was going on. Mum had announced she was marrying Freddie by then and had come to say that she was taking me away, to live with her and her new husband. I watched and listened through the crack of the living room door.

'He's my son and he's coming with me!' Mum shouted.

'He's going nowhere,' Grandad yelled back. 'This is his home, and this is where he's staying!'

The row continued back and forth, and I found myself looking from one to the other wildly, like a spectator at a tennis match. It was such a mad situation. After a while, I felt I had to say something.

'I'm not going anywhere!' I screamed, stepping into the room.

At that very moment, I think I saw my mum's heart breaking. She gave me such a terrible look. All the energy drained out of her and within five minutes she gave up and left, crying as she went. Mum and Grandad didn't speak for a long time after that, and I was left to live with what I had done.

I continued living with my grandparents, but something changed inside me. The trouble in the family had an effect, although I never admitted it. It made me colder and meaner.

I would only see Mum at the weekends, before she would leave me, to go back to her husband, which was so upsetting. To begin with, I cried every time, until I got hardened to that, too. I felt she had chosen him over me. Really, I was the one who chose, but kids don't think like that.

It was all such a mess, and I was still just a young boy, but ours was not a family that kissed and cuddled. I think what I needed was for someone to put their arms around me and tell me everything would be okay.

But no one did.

2

I STAYED at my grandparents' house until I was 11, by which time I had moved up to Firth Park Senior School. At that point, I started to spend more time at Mum's because she lived closer to the school. By then, she had two new kids with Freddie. Of course, that pissed me right off. I was jealous of them all because I felt like I always got pushed to one side. I was just a wounded young man with a bad attitude.

From the beginning at Firth Park, I deliberately set out to make friends with the tough kids. It was the law of the jungle and I saw things in very simple terms. As far as the 11-year-old me was concerned, you were either one of the bullies or you got bullied. That was fine. I was more than happy to terrorise others if it prevented me being terrorised.

I hooked up with a kid called Darren Wright, whose family were from Attercliffe, like mine, and had moved to the same area as us. He introduced me to another kid called Pete. The three of us bossed the playground, became a tight group and often went to hang out at Longley Park, which had an open-air swimming baths. We would spend most of the summer there, just larking around.

Pete's family were wealthier than ours and coincidentally lived in a big house with a garden which backed on to the park. They even owned a boat and a couple of canoes, which blew my mind. Darren and I were council estate kids. Who the hell owned a boat?

One night, Pete invited us to sleep in a tent on his lawn, which we all thought was a great laugh. Darren and I were messing about as usual, until about two in the morning, when Pete's mother came down for the umpteenth time, and told us to go home because of how much noise we were making. Darren had a great idea though. Rather than go home we should get one of the canoes and take it down to the open-air swimming baths. Game on.

We nicked a canoe, went through the park, jumped over the fence by the pool, passed the canoe over, then sailed it up and down until the early hours, running, swimming, laughing and generally being reckless kids. That soon turned into our regular thing.

Word got around and we started to invite other kids to our night-time swimming parties. Small crowds would turn up with anything that would float. Inner tubes, dinghies, you name it. Often there were more kids in that pool at night than there had been in the daytime.

But towards the end of the summer, it all went wrong. One night, as we walked towards the pool we heard voices, then climbed over the fence and saw a bunch of kids none of us knew.

'What do you lot think you're doing here?' Pete asked.

One of them replied, 'Same as you.'

One of our crowd shouted back, 'This is our party, fuck off!'

And that was that.

They ran at us. We stood our ground, and a big fight broke out. Even though it was a light evening, I had to try to focus my eyes, to see if I knew any of them, but I didn't. The cheeky shits had to have it, but there were no potential weapons lying around, only blown-up tbues, and it's tough to do someone much damage one of those.

As we all came together, I got a smack in the face and found myself trying to fight this kid barefoot. We always left our clothes outside the pool in case we needed a quick getaway, to avoid the park patrol who came around on motorbikes. All I had on was a pair of cut-down jeans.

This kid and I went hell for leather, winging punches at each other. He caught me a couple of times, I swung wildly back, lost my balance and ended up falling in the deep end. I was not the greatest swimmer, panicked and somehow scrambled out.

As we headed home, we vowed to be back the next night ready for them, if they turned up again.

So, the following evening we all got together and planned what we were going to do. This time, for a start, I wouldn't be barefoot.

Even though I was still limping, somebody was going to get it, but as we walked through the park, we saw car lights. There seemed to be lots of activity near the pool.

We got to the top of the hill, looked down and saw the park crawling with police. Even we were not stupid enough to head down there and get nicked, so we returned home with a sense of deflation. We later found out someone had broken into the small shop by the pool, stolen the sweets, then set fire to the building. We never found out who did it. Maybe it was the same kids we had the fight with, but that was the end of our great summer in Longley open-air pool. We would have to find something else to do.

Soon, some genius came up with the idea that all of us should get a tattoo, like a gang thing. There was a guy on the Flower Estate who tattooed people in his house, a pretty shonky set-up by all accounts, but we reckoned he was the type of guy who would do it even though we were still just 11 years old.

Nonetheless, on arrival, all of us were a bit taken aback by how filthy his house was. There were dogs and cats everywhere and piles of rubbish in corners. He took us in the back room and demanded money up front, so we all paid him. For some reason, we opted for a simple swallow design on our forearms. I don't know why. It was very unoriginal.

I learned later that the swallow is meant to denote that you have 'done bird' or been to prison. None of us knew that, though. We just thought it would make us look tough.

Darren went first, saying he wasn't scared. After the tattooist completed the black outline on Darren, he asked who was next. I asked why he had not done the colours.

'I'm going to do everyone's black outline first,' he said.

'Aren't you supposed to change the needle for each person?'

'Listen, son. Don't tell me how to do my fucking job, okay?'

Not wanting to miss out on this fantastic opportunity, the other lads all told me to shut up, so I sat down to have my black outline done.

As he worked, I surveyed the tattooist's arms, which were covered in designs. Every one of them was shit. Not a good sign.

I shut my eyes and waited for the pain to end, while straining not to show any reaction on my face. Tough kids don't show weakness, right?

One by one, he went through the group of us, never changing the needle. Last in line was a kid called Dave, and after the tattooist began on him, Dave immediately went pale and started shaking and sweating.

It was funny to begin with but then we all looked at each other anxiously as Dave started to kick his legs out and thrash around.

'What the fuck's wrong with him?' the tattooist asked.

No one had a clue what was going on and some of us began to laugh nervously, as Dave's whole body began jerking and spasming. He knocked into the table holding all the tattoo equipment, sending it flying everywhere. The tattooist looked completely bewildered, which made us laugh even more, until his huge, heavily tattooed wife came in and started shouting.

It was chaos. One of us yelled to call an ambulance, but the woman waved her massive arms around and screamed, 'Don't get no fucking ambulance, get him out of my house!'

The dogs all started barking, cats were running around, and the atmosphere was so crazy it was like a scene from some mad TV show.

I tried to hold Dave's leg, but he was still kicking and flailing, and it was impossible. At that point, Darren and I looked at each other and made a silent joint decision to leave. We pushed to get to the door with this enormous woman shouting that we had to take Dave with us. We just barged our way out and ran down the road laughing our heads off.

Dave, it emerged, had suffered a seizure. But we were 11 and had no idea what that was. It didn't seem especially important, somehow.

The next day we all went to school in short-sleeved shirts, proudly displaying our new, badly rendered tattoos. Eleven years old and all with dirty blue swallows on our arms. We thought we looked the business.

3

FROM 11 to 16, on the days I did go to school, I was always in trouble. Teachers hated me because I messed about non-stop. It soon got to the point that nobody was very bothered if I didn't go in. I think most of the teachers preferred it, in truth.

Truant officers never came to check on me and Mum could not make me go, despite her best efforts. I would just refuse. There was nothing she could do and that was that. As a result, by my early teens I got into a routine of staying up all night and sleeping most of the day – a proper layabout.

Like many teenage lads, I was attracted to anything a bit naughty. Surprisingly, drink and drugs did not draw me in much, though. The first and only time I got drunk was at the back of a local pub called The Pheasant. We loved that place because they used to have strippers on Friday and Saturday nights. We would climb on the windowsills to peek inside at all the boobs and arses. Fabulous. There was no PornHub in the 1970s so that was about as thrilling a view as a teenage boy could get.

One night down there, my older cousin Peter gave us something to drink. Neither Darren nor me knew what it was, but we drank it anyway, then asked for some more. Peter and his mates, who were inside, thought it was great to see us getting drunk and in no time, we were off our heads. We climbed up to watch the strippers and Darren started banging on the window to try and get their attention, so one of the barstaff came out to move us on.

We could not even walk straight and stumbled off, feeling that blurry buzz and hazy headed feeling. We went along Hatfield House Lane and noticed two kids on the other side of the street. I knew them both from school, but not their names, and made up an excuse to ask them why they were looking at us, then whacked one of them in the mouth, just for the hell of it. That's the sort of kid I was.

The next thing I knew, they were kicking the shit out of me, and I was helpless, more or less. I could not stand up, walk or fight back. Eventually, the fight petered out and Darren and I were sat on the pavement laughing at each other, even though we had just been beaten up by two younger kids.

The next morning, I looked like I had been hit by a lorry. I had cuts and gravel under my skin from where they had dragged me along the ground, and bruises all over my back. I reflected on what had happened and although I had quite enjoyed the feeling of being drunk, I definitely did not like the results. That was it for me and alcohol. I had decided that it wasn't for me.

By our mid-teens, when other kids around us were getting into drugs or going through the car-stealing phase, we were still just a general bunch of scallywags. Not that I want to excuse our behaviour. We were pretty horrible in our own way, but there was never any intention within our gang to move into serious criminality. We were just teenage boys, in a post-industrial city, having fun.

There was a period when we spent a lot of time hanging around by the canal down in the centre of Sheffield. Back then, it was a derelict area with old buildings that we treated as a sort of adventure playground, running around, jumping from one bit of wall to the next. Climbing up on window ledges, all that stuff.

One day, we saw a boat moored down on the water. A look led to a suggestion, which led to action, and we all climbed on. Before we knew it, one of us had untied the docking line and we were drifting down the canal, laughing our heads off. We took turns at steering, and were crashing into everything, before Pete decided to push me off the side. After a bit of panic and a lot of splashing about, I managed to get back on the boat. It turned into a game of revenge after that, with all of us being thrown off repeatedly and climbing back on.

That tired us out, especially as it was a warm day, so for a while we just laid there sunbathing on the deck, as the boat floated along, following the current. At one point, some old men fishing on the bank clocked what was going on and started shouting at us, but we just shouted back and made rude gestures. Eventually we floated all the way to Attercliffe, which I recognised, although it looked so different from the boat.

Soon after that, we turned a kind of corner on the canal and were confronted with a fork. As far as we were concerned, it was a straight toss-up, so we took the route to the left. Wrong choice. We cursed our luck as we found ourselves heading for a small waterfall.

It was only about six feet high, so we decided to just hang on and hope for the best. We sailed over the edge, and for a glorious few seconds thought we had pulled it off, but then the boat crashed down and began to roll, so we all panicked and jumped off. We swam to the bank and watched as the boat partially righted itself, although it was clearly damaged. What did we care? We'd had our fun with it and that was all that mattered.

Soaking wet, we decided to head home, but got no further than a hundred yards from the river before a police car pulled up. We were taken to Attercliffe Police Station and left to sit in our wet clothes for ages, until a copper so fat it looked like he would burst out of his shirt gave us a telling-off. He let us go with a stern warning. A lucky escape, and one which signposted the end of us as sailors.

Among our general mischief, we often scrapped too. Not only were we playground bullies and known faces in the area, but we play-fought with each other all the time. For some reason, which I never understood, there were three boxing gloves at my mum's house. A pair and another random one. Every night at 9.25pm, mum used to go to Shiregreen Working Men's club, have a few drinks and come home with my stepdad just after 11.30.

More often than not, as soon as mum went out, a bunch of my mates would come over, and we would sit about smoking and cracking jokes. Then, the three boxing gloves would come out.

In each match-up, whoever was the worse fighter had to wear two gloves and could use both hands, while the other person had to wrap a towel around his spare hand, which he was not supposed to use. Then we would push all the furniture back to the walls, and the evening of fisticuffs would start. I even made my younger half brother and sister fight each other for the pleasure of my mates. That lounge was like the Colosesum of Rome.

One night, I was boxing Peter. He got me up against the wall and started piling in with both hands. I panicked, forgot I only had a towel wrapped round my left hand, hit him with it and sent him to the floor with blood pouring from his nose. We all stood there laughing as he tried to get the gloves off to stop his nose bleeding, running everywhere, claret pouring from his face like a cartoon character. It went all over Mum's carpet, and it was pretty obvious his nose was broken. Naturally, none of us cared. The poor kid was sobbing in pain, and we all just fell about laughing.

Following a couple of years of that sort of thing, the first sign of anything that could be called actual boxing came into my life when I was 14. We were told there would be a boxing competition in school, which was set to take place during PE lessons. Me and my mates all thought this was a great idea. We believed we could fight and without doubt we would smash everyone to bits.

The school did not have a boxing ring, so they got some ropes and tied them across the gym from the wall bars. The area was about 30ft by 10ft. We all lined up and the teacher picked me to fight a kid called Philip Josephs. He was the same age as me, but in a different class.

I stepped forward and smirked at all my mates hanging off the wall bars.

'Go on, Glyn!' they shouted. 'Smash him up!'

I loved the feeling of being the centre of attention. Philip stared at me as the teacher told us to come to the middle of the makeshift ring to shake hands.

'He looks serious,' I thought. 'He must know what I'm going to do to him.'

The bell rang for the first of three rounds, and I came out, determined to get him out of there, windmilling with all my might. Philip danced around me on quick feet, moving his head constantly. I was unable to land a single shot.

By the end of the first round, I had blown my beans. All the swinging had worn me out. I could not get my breath and as I looked at all my mates, still shouting off the wall bars, I thought, '*This ain't funny anymore.*'

My friend, who was working as my chief second, tried to give me water, but I couldn't drink because I was too busy trying to breathe. The teacher shouted for the second round.

You've got to be kidding, I thought. I've only just sat down.

My mate in the corner had to push me off the stool to restart the contest. Out of a sense of duty, I lumbered towards Philip and tried to put my hands up, but he could have knocked me over with a feather.

I had no idea that three minutes could be so long. Philip seemed to know what he was doing. He swatted my head back and forth like a game of swing-ball and there was nothing I could do about it. It would have been better if he had knocked me out cold or forced the teacher to stop it, but he just kept peppering away at me. It was relentless and embarrassing.

By the end of the bout, I had a fat lip and a sore nose, but worst of all, my pride was hurt. I felt like crawling into a hole. My mates were still laughing as I shuffled off to the changing rooms. I did not find out until a little later, but it turned out that Philip boxed for Croft House Amateur Boxing Club, had got his amateur card and already had a few fights under his belt.

I went straight home to sulk after that and did not surface for a while, staying away from school, but I kept thinking about Philip Josephs and how easy it was for him to take me to the cleaners. He didn't look like the toughest lad in the world and if I had come across him in the street, I would have fancied my chances, but the truth had been so different.

Quietly, to myself, I had to admit that I respected that. He played with me, beat me with ease and I think that triggered something in my mind.

4

I LEFT school in 1976, although 'leaving school' is too grandiose a phrase as I virtually never went anyway. I was given an appointment to see the careers teacher, who smiled patronisingly, and asked what I was thinking of doing. I shrugged. I had no qualifications and no real idea.

Inspired by my grandad's past, I went down to the army careers office, where I passed the medical, but was turned down because I did not have a single O-level or CSE to my name.

I couldn't even get in the army. I thought anyone could get in the army. What a kick in the nuts.

It began to dawn on me that maybe, just maybe, I might have messed things up a bit. I found myself having to report to the unemployment office once a week. Those were the rules back then. I couldn't sign on the dole because I was too young, but as a school leaver, they tried their best to get me a job.

The woman at the Job Centre asked me the same question as the school careers advisor. 'What do you want to do?'

'I don't know,' I replied.

'Do you have any qualifications?'

'Nope.'

'What are your hobbies?'

'I don't have any.'

'What sort of things are you interested in outside of school?'

'Nothing.'

She pursed her lips and stared at me over her glasses. 'I see.'

I was still living with my grandparents at Firth Park, but nana wasn't happy. She was an old-fashioned woman and thought it brought shame on our house that I wasn't working. She used to say, 'Why don't you go down to the Labour Exchange to look for work?'

She thought we were still living in the 1930s.

I used to think, 'Are you kidding, nan? There's no work in me.'

But that woman in the Job Centre was determined to get me work. Every week she nagged me about this or that thing she thought I could do. I got the impression she wanted to get rid of me.

One day, she said, 'Glyn, look here, a lovely job for you.'

I had already told her I didn't want a job inside because it would be too much like being back at school.

'What is it?' I asked.

'Window cleaning. Nice, outdoor work. Summer's on its way and I think it will suit you perfectly.'

I snorted with derision. She had to be winding me up. Up and down ladders with a squeegee? Glyn Rhodes? Not a chance.

But she was persistent if nothing else. 'I'll call the employer now for you, Mr Rhodes.'

She phoned the guy, gave him my name and address, and arranged everything. I was to be picked up for my first day at the roundabout in Chapeltown on Monday morning at 8.30. I thanked her and left, sneering inwardly. I had absolutely no intention of being anywhere other than in bed at that time.

When I got home, nan asked, 'Did you get a job today, love?'

'No,' I said solemnly. 'There were no jobs for me today.'

The weekend came and went, and on Monday morning I was woken up by a knock on the front door. Soon, nan was shouting up the stairs.

'Glyn, get yourself down here, there's a man here for you. He says you were supposed to have met him in Chapeltown at 8.30 to start your new job.'

I jumped out of bed in disbelief that this idiot had come all the way from Chapeltown to look for me. As I came down the stairs, he was standing at the bottom, a pleasant-looking fellow in overalls. 'Hello, Glyn,' he said, chuckling. 'Did you not set your alarm clock?'

'Oh yes,' I replied. 'I didn't hear it go off.'

Nan gave me a right look.

So, that was my first job. Glyn Rhodes, window cleaner extraordinaire. I stuck it out for a while and it wasn't too bad, but as soon as the weather got cold, I told the guy I had another job. Of course, I didn't really have one and told my grandmother I had been laid off for the winter.

So, it was back to the Job Centre for me. I'm sure they were ever so glad to see me.

There followed another period of not much, just loafing about, before something came along which changed my life forever. 1976 was a big year for Britain. Punk rock ripped up the charts, there was a crazy heatwave and a serial killer called the Yorkshire Ripper started racking up victims. It was an even bigger year for me.

There was a boxing club not too far from where I lived, held in a church hall in the Wincobank area, called St Thomas' Boxing Club. The sign on the wall outside professed training times to be weekdays between five and seven and on Saturdays between one and three.

Of course, to me and my group of friends, who all fancied ourselves as hardcases, boxing had a certain appeal. You would not have got us down to the sports centre for a nice game of badminton, but boxing training? My pals were all up for that and it became something we talked about a lot.

After getting my fingers burnt by Philip Josephs at school, I was a little reluctant to stick my hand in the fire again, but the gang decided to join the boxing club as a group. Like a sheep, I went along with them.

We made our way there on a Friday and pushed open the door. It felt like stepping off the street into another world. The room was just a regular church hall, with a stage at one end, but there was a boxing ring set up there. As we walked in, there were kids all over the place with an Irishman standing at one end, wearing a donkey jacket and boots, shouting instructions.

'Move your feet ... double jab ... come on, side to side, side to side!'

He saw us come in and beckoned us over. I had never met an Irishman in the flesh before and wondered if they all dressed like that. I later found out that this boxing coach, whose name was Brendan Ingle, actually worked as a labourer on building sites during the day. Back then, boxing was still a part-time gig for him.

His accent fazed me a bit, but he had a winning smile and a real warmth. My first impression was that he was slightly crazy. Not in a straitjacket kind of way, but eccentric. Once you had been with him for half a minute, you really felt the force of his character.

He welcomed us as we filed in, then told us all to line up along one side of the ring, to spar. Brendan began pairing us up and while we waited, I saw a kid roughly the same size as me. Straight away, I had a feeling that Brendan would put me in with him.

The lad was called Walter Clayton. He had a flat nose, which should have been a bit of a warning sign. I pulled on some gloves.

'Okay,' Brendan said, in his Irish brogue. 'What's your name then, young man?'

'Glyn.'

'Right then, young Glen, I'll tell you how this is gonna work. It's your first spar, so you can hit Walter, but he can't hit you back.'

That took the pressure off a bit, so I went in, swinging for the fences and tried to knock Walter's block off. Big mistake. I windmilled and lunged but could not land a glove on this kid. He was moving and sliding, bobbing his head, turning me around. When the spar finished, Brendan winked at me.

'Walter's the junior ABA champion,' he said. 'Do you want to learn to fight like that?'

That night I could not stop thinking about it. The way that kid had been able to evade my best efforts, even while disallowed from hitting me back, impressed me enormously. That instinct rose up inside me again. Brendan was right. I did want to be able to do what Walter could do.

It was a huge moment for me, literally the first time in my whole life I had felt that way. I wanted to do this. Before then, I hadn't given two shits about anything.

And so it began.

5

FROM THAT point on, I went back to St Thomas' every day with my mates. Over the next few months, one by one, they all stopped coming. They got girlfriends, they started going to pubs and nightclubs, but not me. I guess I had the bug. I just kept turning up to that old church hall and listening to the crazy Irishman.

Brendan was like a pied piper figure. He was charismatic and funny, and there was something endearing about him. He was rough around the edges too and used language that would be considered offensive today. But we all liked it, really. He had little insults for each of us. When annoyed with me, he always called me thick, which in his Irish accent sounded like 'tick'.

'No, no, not like that, Glen, ya tick bastard.'

For a kid who had left school without a single qualification, it was a cutting jibe. Somehow though, with Brendan, even when he was cursing you, it felt affectionate.

He would take all us kids on long walks around the countryside and just talk and talk. No one had ever really taken me anywhere before.

'I've seen it all before, lads,' he would say, wisely.

While walking, he would ramble on about anything – love, money, music, whatever was on his mind. He told us about his life, too. Brendan was originally from Dublin and had come to England looking for work. He came from a boxing family and his brother had been European amateur champion. Brendan had a decent career himself, as a middleweight, winning more than half of his 33 fights, but had never picked up a title.

He told us that no one had looked after him properly during his boxing career and that to make it in the pros, you needed a good manager and promoter, people who would protect your best interests. Brendan reckoned he could have picked up a few belts but was often thrown into fights at late notice or given the wrong fights at the wrong times.

'This is how it all works, lads,' he would say. 'It's not just about being good inside the ropes, you've got to be good outside them, too.'

One of the most startling things about Brendan was that he had a way of knowing things that were going to happen before they did. Some new kid would turn up in the gym and look fantastic. The rest of us would be in awe, but Brendan would have a quiet look and say under his breath, 'No, he'll do nothing. Not the right sort.' Sure enough, within a couple of weeks, the talented kid would get bored and quit.

It was as if he had a kind of boxing sixth sense. I thought there was something a bit magical about him.

I had been training with him for a few months when he finished a Friday session by saying, 'Okay, boys, don't come to the gym tomorrow, meet me at the top end of Sheffield Road. We've got some secret training to do.'

When we all turned up at the meeting point the next day, he walked us to his allotment, where he got us all building a wall. Secret training in Brendan's language was basically a codeword for cheap labour, but somehow, none of us minded, even workshy little bastards like me.

As my boxing became more serious and developed into my main interest, it brought me closer to Grandad, too. I think he liked me doing it and started telling me about when he boxed in the army. He would often ask how training had gone and I would talk about the shadow boxing and warm-ups, how we practised footwork on the lines, (which we painted ourselves during one secret training session), all the sparring with the other kids. He loved hearing about it, and I think a part of me was thrilled to get his approval. Nana was completely different. As far as she was concerned, boxing was a massive waste of time.

'Haven't you got a job yet?' That was her daily question.

But I wasn't interested in jobs, I was excited by what I was doing. I learned fast. Brendan taught me well, in a very orthodox style, hands up, move your feet, move your head, work off the jab. After a few months of listening to Brendan, figuring out the basics, especially footwork, he took me to one side.

'Glen,' he said. I'd got used to him calling me Glen by then. 'I've got yous a fight.' It was the first time he said that to me.

He sorted me a medical with an Irish doctor a few doors down from the gym and told me I was booked to fight in Leeds at the Meanwood Working Men's Club.

There were a few of us on the show and after meeting at the gym, Brendan drove us all there in his old VW Camper van. He had an 8-track recorder in the van and was blasting all these old Irish tunes by groups like Foster and Allen, while he sang along at the top of his voice. The whole thing felt like an experience. We weren't just any boxers. We were Ingle boxers.

Altogether, I had 30 amateur fights and did okay. I won my first ten before I started picking up the odd loss. I never won any titles, and even got stopped a few times, but referees in the amateurs tended to jump in very quickly.

More than anything I loved all the trips here and there. Before I met Brendan, I had barely been outside Sheffield, but as a boxer I travelled around regularly, seeing new places, meeting new people. One time Brendan took us down to London for a show and I met the world welterweight champion, John H. Stracey. It blew my mind that he would stop and talk to me. The champion of the whole world. My horizons were broadening.

The highlight of my amateur boxing career was going to Germany with Brian Anderson, who later went on to be British middleweight champion. The best thing about it was that my opponent didn't turn up, so I got a little holiday for free.

Another occasion when I didn't actually box also proved to be especially significant during that time. I was taken as a 'spare' to a show in Chesterfield at a nightclub called the Aquarius. That meant I was not slated to fight, but if someone around my weight dropped out, I would step in.

That night, there was a black kid on the bill, a Nottingham lad fighting for Radford Boys' Club. He was simply the most sensational fighter I had ever seen. He had a big, afro hairstyle as was fashionable at the time, with blue velvet shorts, blue Adidas boots and a white vest. He really looked the part, but what truly blew me away me was how he fought.

He had an incredible hands-down, reflex-based defence. His movements were fluid, graceful and athletic, and he seemed equally comfortable coming forwards or backing off. He could hit out of the orthodox or southpaw stance and you felt like you never quite knew what he would do next, as if he was being spontaneous and making it up as he went along.

This unpredictable, elusive style was so different to the high-guard, chin-down approach that Brendan had taught us. As I watched from ringside, my mouth hung open in shock. I made a mental note of the name – Herol Graham.

A few months later, I walked into the gym on a Sunday morning as usual and stopped short. Herol was there, in the middle of a pad session with Brendan. He looked just as good as he had that night in Chesterfield, and it was clear Brendan was enjoying working with him.

Brendan never told me how it happened, but I always assumed the savvy Irishman must have recognised the kid's talent and poached him. He became part of the furniture in no time.

The funny thing was, that as Herol spent more time in the gym, his style began to rub off on the other lads, including me. Not that we could do it as well as him, but slowly and surely, the Herol Graham style became the gym style. We started to hold our hands low, dance in and out of range and switch between orthodox and southpaw.

At shows, with all the St Thomas' boys fighting like that, people naturally concluded that Brendan must have taught us that way, that all these cocky fancy-dans coming out of his gym were products of his boxing philosophy, but that was not really the case. It was the Herol Graham effect.

Brendan was so proud of his prize asset and wanted to build his profile as much as possible, so came up with an innovative promotional idea of going around working men's clubs every Sunday. A bunch of us would get in his van and tour the clubs, boxing little exhibitions and spars on the dancefloor in front of all the drinkers. His party piece, towards the end of each performance, was to get volunteers from the audience to come up and try to hit Herol.

Herol would put his hands behind his back and dance around, while a queue of beer-bellied middle-aged blokes took turns swinging at him. Herol genuinely enjoyed this and would put on quite an act, sticking out his tongue, making faces and getting the volunteers to make absolute fools of themselves. He would have everyone roaring with laughter.

Before long, Herol won the Amateur Boxing Association middleweight title, making him our gym's first senior, national champion. That gave Brendan some real kudos. People were talking about Herol as a future superstar and obviously that reflected well on the man who trained him. It also reflected well, to some degree, on the rest of us. St Thomas' was developing an aura.

Then, in 1979, with our club really making a name for itself, the ABA suddenly decided to cause us some trouble. Brendan had a mix of fighters, from kids and amateurs like us, up to a handful of pros. At the time, there was nobody very notable and Brendan's best-known professional fighter was a big-hitting super-welterweight called Mick Mills, but the ABA looked into the situation and declared that this contravened their regulations. Amateurs and pros were not supposed to train together back then, so they banned Brendan from amateur competitions.

It was a bit of a blow to the gym and there was a short period of uncertainty. Eventually, Brendan got all us regulars together, explained what had happened and said that if we wanted to continue boxing with him, we had to turn professional.

Up to then, I thought you had to be a top amateur to turn pro. In many ways, I did not really understand the difference between amateurs and pros. The only thing I understood was that professionals got paid, but that started a thought process. Grandad liked me boxing and grandma wanted me to have a job. What if boxing could be my job? As an idea, it seemed to tick a lot of boxes. I was still only 19 years old.

6

MY FIRST pro fight took place in Liverpool at the Adelphi Hotel. I boxed six two-minute rounds against a kid called John Lindo and lost on points, although I was sure I had done enough to win. I banged both my hands up badly and had to take a bit of time off afterwards.

The defeat and the smashed hands were compensated by the fact that I earned £100, which was a fair amount of money in 1979. I had never earned £100 in my life before.

As I started out on my professional journey, I had no major ambitions as a boxer. Perhaps this was not the right way to think about it. I had no real belief that I would be a champion or anything but thought that if I could earn money like this regularly, it would do for now until something better came up.

That £100 did not last long, so after a few days I told Brendan I wanted to fight again and he lined me up to box a guy called Mark Osborne in Doncaster, just two weeks after my debut.

My hands were still killing me, so I spent most of the fight running around the ring jabbing and moving. For some reason, I started taking the mickey out of my opponent, making faces, talking rubbish. It was just one of those spontaneous things you do in the moment. I noticed this got the crowd wound up, which I liked, so I did it even more.

I don't know if my shenanigans got to Osborne, but I won a comfortable four-round decision, despite a woman at ringside shouting abuse at me all the way through. Afterwards, in the changing room, I was sitting on a chair with my gloves still on, feeling pretty pleased with myself, when the door burst open and the woman from ringside ran in. She rushed over and started smacking me around the head, while everyone else in the changing room stood and watched. Eventually, some blokes pulled her off. She was clearly drunk and shouting all kinds of nonsense about my showboating.

'You don't get to come here and behave like that, you bastard!'

The next day I was featured on the front page of the *Sheffield Star*, with the headline 'Local boxer beaten up by irate aunt'. Fame at last. It took me a pretty long time to live that down.

From there, it was fight after fight for a while. No real planning went into things. I took fights as Brendan offered them and looked on boxing as a job that I enjoyed. Something

I could do, that earned me a few quid and wasn't a total pain in the arse.

I stopped a kid called Steve Sims in Stoke, who later went on to be British champion, and had a few other decent wins. The show-off style I premiered against Osborne became a regular feature of my fights, earning me the nickname 'Showboat'. I also discovered I had decent power. I was tall for a lightweight and when I sat down on my punches I could hurt guys, especially at full or three-quarter range. They say that power is the one attribute in boxing that you can't teach, so I must have just had that in me. I don't know where it came from. Maybe Grandad's genes had something to do with it.

On the other side of the coin, I also learned that I could be hurt, too. My eighth fight was in Nottingham, against a very average kid called Kevin Sheehan. I should never have lost to him in a million years, but he came out swinging, caught me cold and knocked me out in the first round. What was strange and also a little bit scary, was that punch shut my brain down for a while, as if Sheehan pressed the off button on my internal computer.

Afterwards, I remembered walking to the ring, remembered the bell going, remembered Sheehan walking towards me, then the next thing I knew I was back in the changing room with Brendan moaning at me for being sloppy.

I had to ask to find out what had happened and was told I had been counted out by the ref. Apparently, I got to my feet well enough and walked from the ring through the crowd to the backstage area. Along the way, people had spoken to me, and I had responded. We had returned to the dressing room, the gloves had come off, I showered and had begun to get changed, but I didn't remember any of that stuff, at all. There was nothing there but blankness. It was as if 20 minutes or so of my life had simply disappeared. The experience shook me up. It's common sense anyway, but it showed me, on a deep, instinctive level that getting knocked out is really bad for your brain. I promised myself I wouldn't let that happen too often.

It took me four months to clock up my first ten fights, winning seven of them, before Brendan told me he had a contest for me against Jackie Turner, a former two-time ABA champion in London.

'But listen, Glen,' he said. 'The fight's over eight rounds.'

I shrugged. The extra distance didn't bother me at all. All I cared about was the larger pay-cheque. Nonetheless, I boxed with the extra time in mind and tried to pace myself.

At the end, I lost on points but was not impressed with Turner. I felt I had showed him too much respect and been overly cautious. The guy had the punching power of a top-class ballerina.

I told Brendan to get me in with Jackie Turner again as soon as possible. I wanted to put that one right. While waiting for the rematch, I won a few, lost a few and continued carving out a little niche for myself. The boxing world wasn't too sure what to make of me.

In January 1981, I fought a guy called Brian Snagg in Liverpool. Snagg was a tough, come-forward, rough-housing fighter, so I pulled out the full repertoire of tricks to put him off. As usual, my antics made a big impact with the crowd.

As the third round ended, Snagg and I were clinching in his corner. The bell rang and his seconds prepared for the interval so, for a laugh, I sat on his stool. Snagg was not impressed and shoved me off with both hands, which the crowd loved. I stood up and made a gesture of bemusement and offence. The audience roared with laughter. It was like Laurel and Hardy.

I had so much fun, until the end, when the ref gave the decision to Snagg on points. I wasn't sure that was entirely fair, but, as I walked from the ring, I was treated as if I had just won a world title. I signed hundreds of autographs. Reporters clamoured to talk to me in the changing room.

The following day's *Liverpool Echo* filed this report on my performance:

THAT'S ENTERTAINMENT
...The Atkinson brothers' promotion turned out to be a great night's entertainment, thanks largely to a magnificent final bout featuring a sort of white man's version of Frazier versus Ali.

An eight-round lightweight contest in Liverpool watched by an audience quaffing lager from the can, might not have the glamour of the Thrilla in Manila. But with Glen (Glyn) Rhodes, a 20-year-old extrovert cast in the role and Liverpool's Smoking Brian Snagg in opposition, the action was both dramatic and hilarious.

Snagg, a strong, sturdy, bullish figure ploughed forward relentlessly throughout the eight rounds.

Rhodes, who arrived in the ring clad in a full-length black robe, danced and joked his way through, infuriating the spectators by constantly taking the mickey out of his opponent.

Catching Snagg with a full-blooded right, which made a noisy contact, Rhodes stopped in his tracks and inspected his right glove as if in disbelief.

Then, wriggling away from an awkward situation against the ropes, he mopped his brow in mock relief, winked to the crowd and grinned indulgently at Snagg.

It was a laugh a minute, but as the motto on the trainer's jersey said, 'There's just one Snagg' and Rhodes lost on points.

For me, he was a winner in entertainment value, but I should imagine while he is a promoter's dream he must be a manager's nightmare.

Indeed, when I called on him in the dressing room, where the smell of Christmas still hung damply in the air, one of his handlers was angrily telling him that he would have won if he had only fought like an ordinary boxer.

'But I don't want to be an ordinary boxer. I want to be a name people will pay to see,' he replied.

That article pretty much summed me up. I may not have been an ordinary boxer, but when I eventually fought Jackie Turner again, in Mayfair, in London, in my 22nd fight, I meant business.

I climbed into that ring so full of confidence. His amateur pedigree did not matter anymore. The eight-round distance didn't matter anymore. I knew I could beat him.

I walked over to his corner as he was shadow boxing before the first bell, glared at him and said, 'I'm going to fucking knock you out.'

Turner's famous old trainer, Freddy Hill, heard me say it and was not best pleased, but I was good to my word and smashed the kid to bits in two rounds. Unsportingly, I thought, Hill then reported me to the British Boxing Board of Control (BBBoC) afterwards, saying my 'clowning antics' were detrimental to the game. I thought that was pretty sad of him really. It was clearly sour grapes, and he was just upset that I had hammered his fighter.

As a result of Hill's complaints, Brendan and I had to go to London to appear before the BBBoC and answer questions about my conduct before the fight. It was my first experience of this sort of thing. The middle-aged, podgy officials all sat there with serious faces and asked me to explain myself. It was like being in court.

'I'm very sorry, sir,' I said. 'I honestly don't know what came over me and I promise it won't happen again.'

I was reprimanded for 'ungentlemanly conduct and bringing the sport into disrepute' and had to sit there, listening to their drivel for what felt like an eternity. At last, they asked me to leave the room while they discussed my punishment.

I walked outside to find Jackie Turner waiting in the corridor with Hill. To be fair to him, Jackie was mortified.

'This wasn't my idea, Glyn,' he said, so I shook his hand, then stared daggers at Hill. Fortunately, after a long period of deliberation, the BBBoC decided no action was warranted, and I got away with a wrist slap for being a naughty boy.

Turner went on to lose a few more after I battered him, then ended up retiring a couple of years later. Maybe I took the wind out of his sails. He proved to be the classic example of a boxing stereotype. The top amateur who simply was not cut out for the pros. Amateurs punch for points. Professionals punch to hurt. Not everyone can make that adjustment.

Throughout this first part of my boxing career, I learned, bit by bit, how the game works. I suppose all fighters do. Every now and then, Brendan would have a word with me, to tell me to take things more seriously. He wanted me to give it everything, but I just wouldn't. I had come to love boxing, but it wasn't in me to devote myself to it, heart and soul.

The truth was I never liked training. My fitness levels weren't great for a professional and although I reached the stage that I could drag myself through eight rounds if I had to, I think Brendan believed that if I got myself in proper shape, I could move up to 10- and 12-rounders and box for titles.

Like anybody, the idea of being a champion appealed to me, and Brendan was an engaging and convincing speaker, so I promised him I would start training. By then, Herol had moved to a house quite near mine, so I said I would go running with him. He was racking up win after win, of course, under his strange nickname 'Bomber'. They had called him that ever since he came up from Nottingham, which was weird. The guy was one of the most beautiful boxing technicians you could ever hope to see, but was not a massive hitter for a middleweight, so I never understood how he got that tag.

Herol and I were good pals and regular sparring partners by then, so it could have worked. I ran with him a couple of times but just could not be bothered to keep it up, so it soon fizzled out.

To a large degree, I guess, that's the difference between a good fighter and an average one. Talent can only take you so far. You need the right attitude and you need belief, and I didn't have those things. Sometimes I wonder if perhaps I needed to be a touch braver. It can be scary to commit yourself to something with everything you've got, because if you come up short, there's no conclusion other than you simply weren't good enough. If you hold back, you've always got an excuse. 'I could have done this and that, but I didn't train.' Maybe I wanted that line to fall back on.

It's not just about being good inside the ring. You need to be good out of it, too.

Despite that, boxing had taken a big hold on me. I started to read books and buy boxing magazines, learning whatever I could about the sport. I always hated reading at school, but as a boxer, it was becoming something I did by choice.

I found a boxing book about an old gym in New York called Stillman's, which fascinated me. I read about Madison Square Garden, where so many great fights had happened, and I made my mind up, just like that, that I would go there.

A friend of mine from the gym called Neil Jordan was similarly enthused, so I had a few more fights, saved up the money and Neil and I booked tickets.

I was wide-eyed at the whole experience. We landed at JFK Airport and got in a famous yellow cab. We stayed in a hotel in Times Square and did all the usual tourist stuff. We went up the Twin Towers and the Empire State Building, went to Central Park, the Bronx and Brooklyn. We even went to a circus in Madison Square Garden, just to say we had visited the venue.

In the middle of our stay, we got talking to a guy in the hotel who told us that the featherweight legend, Sandy Saddler, who I had read about in books, now trained fighters in a gym at the Maritime Center, not too far from our hotel.

The idea of meeting such a legendary boxer truly excited me and we walked to the address, where we met a sailor-looking type on the way in. He told us Saddler was just inside. As soon as we walked in, I recognised him, having seen his picture in books. Tall and thin, with sunglasses on, he sat on a high stool in a corner of the room.

'Hello boys,' he said as we approached. 'Have you come to see the champ?'

We all shook hands. He seemed genuinely flattered. 'So, you two came all the way from England to see me?'

We told him we had, although that was not strictly true and he immediately began talking about his career, in particular his famous quartet of fights with the legendary Willie Pep. He said for one of their contests, Pep trained with a wrestler and as a result, their fight turned into a wrestling match. He seemed quite bitter towards Pep, going on and on about him for some time, and asking us how Pep could be considered the best featherweight of all time when he had beaten him three times out of four. It was hard to argue much with that.

Nonetheless, Saddler came across as a real, cool character. He was in his late fifties by then but still looked lean and wirily strong. I found him fascinating. We stayed there and talked with him for hours.

The following day, we visited Gleason's Gym, which was such an atmospheric place, exactly how you'd imagine it. An old, spit 'n' sawdust affair, with a cracked front window and heavy bags that looked like they had been strung up in the twenties. A guy in a suit introduced himself as the manager and told me I could only take pictures if I paid $20, because lightweight champion Roberto Duran was coming to train that day.

'Fair enough,' I said and paid him the money. I didn't want to upset anyone. We stayed for a while, soaking up the atmosphere until I was approached by someone else.

'Hey buddy, who gave you permission to take pictures in here?' the guy asked.

'The manager,' I told him. 'He said it was $20 because Roberto Duran was coming in.'

The fellow almost had a heart attack laughing. 'I'm the manager,' he said. 'And Duran ain't training today. But if you want to take pictures it's still $20.'

I had to have a little laugh myself. These guys were shaking me down for a few photos. I paid him a 20 too, and we left not long after, before someone else pulled the same stunt.

Welcome to New York, Glyn.

7

BY THE middle of 1981, I was an established pro, I guess, although I was still a boxer who defied definition to some extent. No one knew if I was a contender, a gatekeeper or a journeyman, which suited me fine. I had some ability, though, and that, combined with my growing reputation as an awkward so-and-so who clowned around and enjoyed making opponents look silly, meant Brendan was finding it harder to get me fights. To borrow a line from the famous manager and promoter, Mickey Duff, I was becoming a fully paid-up member of the 'who needs him club'.

Perhaps because of that, a mini-era began in which I boxed on Herol's undercards. It was almost as if I was his chief support act. Brendan's attitude towards me shifted accordingly, I thought. He stopped trying to talk me into taking things seriously and began taking me for granted. Maybe it was fair enough under the circumstances.

I knew, of course, that Herol was the gym star, who everyone expected to be world champ sooner or later, so the main focus was on him. If I am honest though, things started to get tense between myself and Brendan, at times.

Brendan's frustration at my lack of drive sometimes even showed itself during fights. When I boxed the Midlands Area champion, Doug Hill in Staffordshire, Brendan started screaming at me between rounds, going all red in the face, with spit flying from his mouth. He was desperate to get a reaction from me, but I just ignored him and stared into space. People in the first few rows cracked up laughing at the apoplectic Irishman with his disinterested fighter. Everything was like comedy in my career.

In the end I got fed up listening to Brendan's yelling, went for it and stopped Doug Hill in the sixth, with a right uppercut to the body. I did it to shut Brendan up, more than anything.

Later that year, after I boxed a draw with a good kid called Lance Williams, *Boxing News* summarised how the boxing world saw me.

> Rhodes has established himself as the clown prince of pro boxing. It's a tag he revels in; spectators were treated to the full repertoire during the early rounds of this bout with Williams. He shuffled, stuck out his chin and at one point grabbed hold of the top rope with his right glove while fending off Williams with his left. When Rhodes gets down to serious business, he's a tricky, hard-hitting fighter.

Soon I began to get the impression that Brendan's frustration with me had affected the way he managed my career. Not long after Williams, I got one of those standard phone calls.

'Glen, Glen, I've got yous a fight. It's an easy one, just go in there, fiddle around, you'll be fine.'

'Okay,' I said. 'Who and where?'

The kid's name was Vernon 'The Entertainer' Vanriel, a tough character from Tottenham in north London. We boxed at York Hall in Bethnal Green and at the time, Vanriel was hot property, on his way up, gunning for titles. It was anything but an easy fight. Brendan either made a mistake or had misled me. Vanriel was all over me from the start.

I scraped through the first round but at some point, got hit with a body punch which somehow hurt my face. It was game over in the second. He smashed me with a right hook on the cheekbone. I went down, got up, but I was done. The referee called it off.

'Oh, these easy fights,' I said to Brendan in the changing room afterwards. 'Whatever you do, please don't get me any hard ones.' It hurt me to talk.

We drove back to Sheffield in Brendan's old green VW van that had no heating. I sat in the back, freezing, not talking and feeling my face swell up to about twice its normal size. Every time the van went over a bump, pain shot through the injury.

We stopped at some services on the M1 and as we walked in under the lights, Brendan looked sideways at me. I could tell by his expression that he was shocked.

'Bloody hell, Glen,' he said. 'Are you alright?'

That's when I knew I was in trouble. For Brendan to comment like that, it had to be bad.

As soon as we arrived back in Sheffield, Brendan took me to the hospital, where we waited ages for an X-ray. After I had it done, I returned to the waiting area to find Brendan asleep in a chair.

When my name was called to see the doctor, Brendan opened his eyes and said, 'I'm getting off now, Glen, give me a ring tomorrow afternoon, let me know how you got on. Call in the afternoon though, okay? I'll be in bed all morning, I expect.'

I watched him walk out, then stayed in the hospital for several more hours, until they eventually gave me some painkillers and discharged me. It was the middle of the night, and I started to walk home, but had to tiptoe, because every time I put my foot down it hurt my face. The painkillers didn't seem particularly effective.

When I got in, I looked at my face in the mirror and it was gruesome. I looked like a monster from a horror film. 'What the fuck are you doing?' I thought to myself. I felt like Brendan had thrown me to the lions.

Outside the ring, in my early twenties, I remained a free spirit, coming and going as I liked, with no stability at all. I still hung around with the kids I grew up with, doing a bit of this and a bit of that, until the standard thing happened. I met a girl, fell in love, and made an attempt at settling down. It was never likely to work. There was no way I was ready for that sort of commitment, but we had a son together and that meant I needed more money than ever. We had a council house, and after my boy Alex's birth I felt, for the first time, a real need to get my act together, but other than boxing, what could I do?

We arranged our wedding for Saturday, 20 November 1982 and my stag night was on the 18th. Just to keep everything nice and complicated, I was also scheduled to box ten rounds for the Central Area title on Monday, 22 November in Liverpool. As always, I was in Glyn Rhodes style 'hard training'.

My stag night, at a Sheffield nightclub, was a disaster. I was the only one sober at the end of the evening, my friends started a riot and there were bodies everywhere. The owner of the nightclub flipped his lid and said he was reporting me to the BBBoC.

As they do, the wedding cost a fortune. Two Rolls-Royces, big party, all the usual stuff, but the pictures were a good laugh, at least. All the men had black eyes and lumps on their faces. Afterwards it was back home to our council house in the early hours of Sunday morning, with no honeymoon as I was boxing so soon afterwards.

On the Monday I was fighting in Liverpool, against Kevin Pritchard, who went on to become British super-featherweight champion. I was in no mood to mess about and knocked him out cold in the fifth round, with a right uppercut followed by a left hook. I was lucky that he went straight to sleep, as throwing that combination also broke both my hands.

Instead of going home to my new wife, I spent another night in the Royal Hallamshire Hospital and came out with both arms in plaster. At least I was Central Area lightweight champion.

Suddenly, I had a proper title and belt, to go with my wife and child. That gave me pause for thought.

By then, my grandparents had moved from the house I grew up in and lived close quite close to me. I often called in to see them as I was passing, but the state of Grandad in his old age saddened me. He walked with a stick and eventually had to have his leg amputated. Superman wasn't Superman anymore.

This was a guy who lived through the Great Depression of the 1930s, fought in World War Two, then came home to work in the steelworks, never had a day off, retired at 65 and got given a watch. A fucking watch! Then before he had much chance to enjoy his retirement, he suffered a stroke.

When Grandad died, I found myself sitting in their home and looking at what they had. A meagre council house containing a few bits of furniture. That's what you get for being honest, playing by the rules and working hard all your life?

It didn't seem fair.

I defended my Central Area title in March, against a kid called Jimmy Bunclarke from Liverpool. I thought my hands would be better, but I was wrong. Early in the fight, I had Jimmy in all kinds of trouble, but he hung in there. By the fourth, my hands were in agony again and I ran out of steam. I forgot about the Queensberry Rules, started fouling and must have hit Jimmy in the balls about ten times, but the referee didn't say a word.

I lost on points, which signalled the end of my short reign as a champion. I would like to be able to say that I was bitterly disappointed, that a fire had been lit inside me, that I vowed to challenge for honours again, but it wouldn't be true. I was more interested in pocketing the purse and thinking about the next one.

I decided to give my hands some time to heal and took another boxing-related holiday, this time to Miami, with the aim of visiting the 5th St Gym where Muhammad Ali had trained as a kid. By this time, Ali had retired and was clearly suffering the effects of his long career, but I had become a huge fan. Like many others, I was drawn to the magnitude of his personality and the impact he had outside the sport, just as much as his achievements as a boxer.

The 5th St Gym was a slight disappointment in the end. There was nothing particularly notable about it, other than the fact it was run by Chris Dundee, the brother of Angelo, Ali's former trainer. He told me that Angelo ran another gym in Pembroke Pines, north of Miami, which piqued my interest straight away. I headed up there the following day and after waiting around for a while, found myself like a starstruck schoolgirl when Dundee turned up. I had read and heard so much about him and was genuinely nervous speaking to him, but he was so accommodating. As I was leaving, he said, 'Next time you come over, bring your gear and you can train with me while you're here.'

I walked out of that place feeling ten feet tall. He probably said it to all the kids who went to his gym, but I returned home determined to go back and train with him.

Back in England, all I thought about was getting enough money together to go back to Miami. I saved every penny I could get my hands on, and it was not long before I had enough.

On my return, I was booked into a place called the Wonderful Time Motel. The room had a bed, a fridge, a shower and a fan in the roof, that squeaked all night when it was 100 degrees, but that was all I needed. Angelo Dundee had moved gyms, but the new place was a little closer to where I was staying, so I was happy. When I walked through the door on the first day, he saw me, recognised me immediately, and said, 'So you found us again.'

So that's how Glyn Rhodes, a lightweight from Sheffield, England, with a record of 15 wins, 10 losses and 3 draws ended up training briefly with the great Angelo Dundee. He had fighters there from all over the world, so I had no trouble fitting in. When, after a couple of weeks, the time came to go home, I was disappointed and promised myself I would be back as soon as possible.

MY FIRST fight back in England was against a Welsh kid called Robert Lloyd, at a black-tie event at the Cutlers' Hall in Sheffield. The fight was over eight rounds, and I was a lot fitter than usual after training in Angelo Dundee's gym. Lloyd chased me all over the ring, but I won on points and felt as though I could have carried on for another eight rounds if I wanted to.

Straight after that, I was asked if I would go to Belfast to spar with featherweight star, Barry McGuigan. The 'Clones Cyclone' as he was known, was in training for a shot at the European title. The money was good, so I accepted.

The first day at the gym in Belfast, I found it packed with reporters and photographers, which was strange to me and made it feel more like a fight than a spar. I climbed in the ring, the bell rang for the first round and Barry hit me straight off with his trademark left hook to the body, which winded me. I sank to my knees.

It was the first punch he had thrown. I was mortified.

I sat on the canvas wheezing and trying to get my breath back with all the assembled press wondering who this mug was they had brought over from England. Back on my feet, and with the lesson well learned, I got up on my toes and ran around that ring like a greyhound. There was no way I wanted to get done to the body again.

Barry's trainer, Eddie Shaw, kept shouting, 'Stand still and fight!' He was perfectly entitled to do that, but I felt I was perfectly entitled to ignore him, so I paid him no attention whatsoever.

Nonetheless, training with Angelo Dundee, then sparring with Barry McGuigan, I began to wonder if maybe I had turned some sort of corner? Maybe this would be the time when everything clicked into place, and I started trying to fulfil my potential.

Back home in Sheffield, I told everyone that I would begin training seriously. I felt like the more I said it, the more it would make it real. Plenty of people told me I could be a champion if I knuckled down.

I had only been back a couple of days when Brendan rang.

'Glen, Glen, I've got yous a fight.'

'Where?'

'It's in France.'

I had never boxed in France before, so immediately agreed on that basis. It would be a fun trip. We drove to Dover and got the ferry, then drove some more. Brendan spent the whole journey talking and talking, as was his habit. He had always been a great speaker and I loved listening to his stories, but interestingly, despite the hours of chin-wagging he did, he never found the right moment to tell me the kid I would be boxing was the French champion. It must have slipped his mind.

On the evening of the fight, the referee came into our dressing room. He said in English, 'I am your referee,' then started to tell me, at length, all the basic rules of boxing, like going to the neutral corner if I knocked my opponent down, not hitting below the belt and so on. He went on and on until I almost fell asleep. Why was everyone taking it in turns to chew my ear off?

Once in the ring, they introduced my opponent as Frederic Geoffroy, who had 14 straight wins to his name. The hall was full, and the crowd seemed very excitable.

'Hello,' I thought. 'This could be lively.'

In the end, Geoffroy and I had a real up-and-downer. I floored him twice and went down three times myself, before the ref stopped me in the fifth, but the whole trip took a bit of the shine off, in some ways. The excitement of Miami and the possibility of achieving something in the game felt further away again. I was back to the old Glyn, taking short-notice fights with limited chances of success, and was not too happy with Brendan.

That feeling soon doubled when I fought at the Royal Albert Hall in London. I was excited to box at such a prestigious venue, but there was traffic on the way down, we arrived late and as we walked through the door, the whip said, 'Glyn Rhodes? You're on at 7.30pm.'

It was 6.45, so I had just 45 minutes to get ready after spending more than four hours sitting in Brendan's VW Camper. I barely got my kit on by the time I was called and soon, I found myself walking back to the changing room having just been stopped in the first round, by a kid called Mo Hussein.

That was my 32nd fight and meant my record was as mixed as possible. Sixteen wins, 13 losses and three draws. I felt silly that I had gone around telling everyone that I was taking things seriously. Future champ? Who was I kidding?

Despite that, when I knocked out a fighter called Willy Wilson, in October 1984, in Nottingham, after virtually no training, Brendan phoned and said he had got me another crack at the Central Area lightweight title. It was scheduled for the City Hall in Sheffield, which made me very happy, as I could bring a hometown crowd for once. I celebrated by booking a holiday to Spain for the week after the fight. My plan was to win back my old title, bank the purse, then have two weeks soaking up the sun afterwards as a reward.

That plan got disrupted when we were informed that the show had been postponed. There was no information yet as to when the rescheduled date would be and as I had the holiday booked, I flew out to the Costa del Sol anyway and worked on my tan.

I arrived back from the holiday on a Tuesday night, called Brendan the following morning and asked if there was a fight date yet.

'Yes, Glen,' he said. 'Funny you should ask. It's this Sunday.'

I could not believe what I was hearing.

'I can't fight ten rounds on Sunday, I only just got back. I've been sitting on my arse for two weeks.'

Somehow, as he always did, Brendan talked me into it. He had a sort of paternal power over me, which carried a lot of weight for a guy who had never known his own father. The one thing in my favour was that I was a natural lightweight and because I didn't drink, I also didn't tend to balloon between fights as some boxers do. That meant there was no question of having to dehydrate myself before the weigh-in.

I prepared by having three sessions in the gym – Wednesday, Thursday and Friday. It was too late to sort out any proper sparring, so I sparred with Brendan, of all people. He was 45 by then but could still do a bit.

In reality though, the truth of all this is a little uncomfortable. At the time, I was not fully aware of it myself, but it's something I came to understand later on. The show that Sunday was an Ingle promotion. Technically, Brendan's wife Alma was the promoter, but everyone knew who was really setting things up. Like any promoter, Brendan needed to sell as many tickets as possible. As a local fighter, with lots of friends, it was important for him and for his financial bottom line that I remained on the rescheduled show. If I pulled out, there was a chance he would make a loss.

The thing that is sometimes difficult to square is that Brendan was my trainer and manager, and also something much deeper than that, a kind of mentor, but in addition to those things, he was a businessman too. He knew that taking a ten-round contest a few days after coming back from holiday was not a good idea for me from a boxing standpoint, but those thoughts were outweighed by his own financial interests.

I boxed a kid called Muhammed Lovelock from Manchester, who was nothing special. I had no real problem handling him, but by the end of the ninth round I was knackered beyond belief. I literally could not hold my hands up.

As I sat in the corner gasping for air, Brendan squirted a bit of water in my face and said, 'Go on, Glen, stay with your boxing. All you have to do is finish on your feet and you're champion again.'

I went out for the tenth like a zombie. Lovelock, on the other hand, knew he was behind on points, so piled in with everything he had. He swung crudely, but it's hard to be evasive when you're exhausted, and he caught me with a massive right hand. It hit me above my left eye; I went down on one knee and felt blood pouring down my face. I got up, but the ref took one look at the cut and stopped the fight. What a sickener.

There were hundreds of people there to see me and, suddenly, the room went quiet.

I sneaked out of the City Hall, utterly humiliated. At home, I sat alone crying, looking in the mirror at the stitches in my eye. Why the fuck did I box a title fight just after coming back from holiday? What sort of idiot does that? I felt like a fool for believing anything else could have possibly happened. It didn't matter what Brendan said. I should have known.

When I finally plucked up the courage to go out, a couple of days later, I had to put up with sarcastic comments from friends and acquaintances, some of whom had bought tickets. Most of them thought they were being funny, but I really struggled with that.

Ever since I walked into Brendan's gym as a 16-year-old, boxing had given me a direction and something to do, but the shame of this defeat and especially the circumstances around it were too much for me. I made a decision to pack it in. I was 25 by then, had been boxing for nine years and felt there was nowhere else for me to go with it.

I put my determined face on and went down to the gym, to see Brendan and tell him the news. I am not sure what I was expecting. This was the 80s and we were men, so I didn't think he would break down in tears, throw his arms around me, or start reciting poetry, but I thought there would be a speech of some kind. He would have a way of giving the moment some depth.

After all, Brendan was never short of things to say, but he listened to me and nodded wearily. He only seemed half interested.

'Okay, well, if that's what you've decided, Glen, fair enough,' he said. 'Nice knowing you an' all.'

That was that.

'Right then,' I said.

So, I turned and walked out.

Glyn Rhodes, ex-boxer. On the street outside I felt a little lump of emotion in my throat. What was I going to do with the rest of my life?

By then, I was divorced, with one child. I had spent any money I had earned. I had no qualifications and no experience in anything other than punching and being punched. What sort of work might that skillset lend itself to?

I looked around and before long got myself a job as a security man at a massage parlour'. Massage parlour was the polite name for it, obviously, as customers came there for much more than a rub-down. My working hours were midnight until 7am. That suited me.

In many ways, it was actually an interesting job. Essentially, I had to keep an eye on who came in the place and ensure they did not start getting rowdy. If they did, I had to turf them out. Simple as that.

It was fascinating to see how the girls went about the work and how some of the men behaved. Of course, a lot of the customers were drunk or high, but there was still something quite telling about it all. It certainly provided a whole new perspective on relationship dynamics. A large percentage of blokes, I concluded, are just arseholes.

All my mates thought it was brilliant and that I had the best job in the world, but it was just a little thing to pay the bills. It kept me busy and paid okay, though. I may even have stuck with it long term, but fate had other ideas.

Eighteen months or so after leaving the sport, I bumped into Herol Graham in the street. It was great to see him again. He told me he had fallen out with Brendan over money. As a result, he had left St Thomas' too, and was in the process of opening his own gym. He was now managed by Irish millionaire Barney Eastwood, who also handled Barry McGuigan. I listened with interest. Herol was one of the few people from the boxing world I still had total respect for. Although he had become a stablemate of mine, I admired him so much. In some ways, he was everything I wished I could have been: dedicated, sharp, gifted, athletic. In my mind, he was everything I was not.

Eastwood had brought over a trainer for Herol from Panama, of all places, called Fredric Plumber and Herol's gym was being set up in a building in the Wicker, an arterial street in Sheffield with railway arches. He said he was looking for help to get the place up and running. When he said that, he raised his eyebrows in invitation.

There was no way I was going to refuse Herol, so I left my knocking shop job and began almost straight away. With a lot of financial help from Graham Longdon, a local jeweller, we managed to get the place looking like a gym. It was on the ninth floor and we had to lug everything up the stairs which was heavy going.

Once the gym was set up, Herol needed sparring. Feelers were put out, but I told him that in the meantime, I would spar with him until they got some proper partners in.

Of course, Herol was out of my league. I couldn't hit him with a handful of pebbles, but in those days neither could anybody else in Europe, so it wasn't a major problem. At least I could present him with a mobile target.

Soon, the gym began attracting attention and people started turning up to watch Herol train. There was a huge amount of local and national expectation attached to his name. He was widely regarded as one of the country's top fighters.

For me, at that point in my life, that was all it took. Just being in a gym every day, sparring regularly and absorbing the excitement around me triggered a familiar reaction. The boxing bug bit me.

Again.

ONCE I made the decision to lace the gloves back on, I had an immediate problem. Brendan was extremely annoyed at losing his golden goose in Herol and was angry at anybody associated with Bomber's new career path. Clearly, I could not go back to Brendan's gym because he knew I was involved.

I was told about a man in Chesterfield called Billy Shinfield. Apparently, he would be able to get me some fights, so I went to see him and liked him. He was a proper, old school boxing character, from a family with bare-knuckle heritage, and after a quick chat he became my new manager.

It was two years since my last fight against Lovelock by then, which is a long lay-off for anyone. Billy said he had a fight for me in Belfast against a debutant, which should be a walk in the park. As usual, I didn't ask too many questions. The wages were good, and that was my main concern. I should have learned my lesson by then.

When I arrived in Belfast, I discovered I was fighting Andy Holligan, a former amateur star from Liverpool who had been lined up to go to the Olympics but chose to turn pro instead. Holligan was widely tipped for great things and essentially, I was the sacrificial lamb brought in to make him look good on his debut. Oh, it was good to be back.

Predictably, it was not the comfortable return to the ring I had been led to believe it would be. I was rusty as hell and Holligan was like a lion going after a meal. He put me down early in the first, then brought the heat from that point on. Survival instincts kicked in, I went into full-on gazelle mode and ran for six rounds after that. Holligan was pulling his hair out, but the crowd loved it and actually threw 'nobbins' in the ring at the end.

Of course, I lost. It had been everything I could do to get through it, but the proceeding passage of time showed my efforts that night to be pretty commendable. Holligan went on to become British and Commonwealth champion and even challenged the legendary Julio Cesar Chavez in Mexico for the world title. Going the distance with him after two years off was not too shabby. Regardless, I was no longer an ex-boxer. 'Showboat' Rhodes was back on the scene.

Back in Sheffield, at the gym, Herol was in the depths of training for a big fight at Wembley Arena in London. He was set to defend the European middleweight title against an Italian fighter of Congolese heritage, called Sumbu Kalambay. Herol had a perfect, 38-fight winning record at that point and if successful against Kalambay was expected to challenge for a world title shortly afterwards. For most people, myself included, there was no doubt that that's where Bomber was headed.

I drove Herol's girlfriend down to London for the fight, which was a little uncomfortable. There had been some problems with their relationship in the build-up, which is the last thing a boxer needs when involved in fights of that magnitude. Once we got into the arena, I noticed Brendan and his wife Alma were sitting a couple of rows back from the ring. I wondered what Brendan's motivation was and suspected that deep down he wanted Herol to lose the fight.

It was Herol's first pro fight without Brendan in his corner, and I wondered what effect it might have on him to see Brendan there. The two of them were estranged and not speaking, and boxing is such a psychological sport. It worried me.

As soon as the fight started, you could tell there was something wrong with Herol. His timing was off and his movement not as slick as usual. Nonetheless, he went the full 12 rounds with a very tough challenger. Towards the end of the fight Herol got hit with a shot that sent him reeling backwards, against the ropes, which prevented him from going down and taking a count. At ringside, I was in shock. Genuine shock. It was unheard of for Herol Graham to get hit like that.

Ultimately, it was a close decision, but Herol lost for the first time. I know Herol was devastated, but he appeared to take it well. That was Herol. To be fair, although he was off form that night, it was another result which does not seem so bad in retrospect. Kalambay beat American slugger Iran Barkley in his next fight to become WBA world champion and then made several successful defences of the world title. Even so, I still think, at his best, Herol would have beaten him.

Afterwards, I was gutted. We returned to Sheffield where the mood in the gym was very down. Herol tried to make everyone feel better, smiling and joking, because that is what he is like, but I knew he was putting on an act. I knew him too well.

After that, there was a strange little period, during which Herol got his career back on track with a couple of good wins, while I boxed on his undercards just like before. He beat an American called Ricky Stackhouse in Doncaster in December 1987. On the same bill I won against a kid called Sugar Gibilru, who went on to become British champion a few years later.

Following that, Herol was slated to box James Cook, a decent Londoner, for the British middleweight title at the City Hall, scene of my big humiliation a few years before. The show was set for June 1988 and of course, I had a spot on the card, too.

Back in the gym, everything had started to feel a bit strange, though. Herol was rarely there, for a start. Myself and a couple of other guys took on most of the coaching work, especially with the kids, as Bomber seemed to have disappeared. The gym was still busy, but it would have been better if he had popped in occasionally to help out.

Slowly, it emerged that Herol had made up with Brendan and started training back at St Thomas'. This was quite a kick in the balls for everyone who had helped him get the gym up and running. It looked terrible. 'Welcome to Herol Graham's boxing gym, but although his name is over the door, he's not here because he trains somewhere else.'

Pretty quickly, Herol's gym fell apart and the business folded. I think Herol felt a little guilty about it all as ultimately, he was the one who had brought me back into the fight game. I had been quite happy minding prostitutes, thank you very much.

He came to speak to me and said that if I intended to continue boxing, I should come back to Brendan's too. At the time, I did not see that I had too much choice. It felt embarrassing to go back like that, but I just had to swallow it.

So, suddenly, there we all were, just like the old days. All the boys and Brendan. It was not the same, though. Few would have noticed, only the close few, but the trust had been eroded. We all had emotional baggage by then, little grievances with each other that festered below the surface.

There were some excellent youngsters in the gym by that point. Fighters I had seen come through at Brendan's as young kids, who were making huge strides. Cruiserweight Johnny Nelson had put a run of wins together after losing his first three fights. Naseem Hamed, still a teenager, was already phenomenal. Ryan Rhodes was a couple of years younger. All of them would go on to have fantastic careers.

Within myself, I promised that now I was back at Brendan's, I would get serious about boxing. I didn't go around telling everyone this time but kept it private. That made no difference and before long I found myself in the same routine as before. I would turn up to train and look through the gym door, to see who was there to spar with. If there was no one worthwhile, I would just turn around and go home.

It was a good little period. I picked up some sponsorship, which was lovely, and had a couple of good wins. I banished my Sheffield City Hall demons by scoring a first-round knockout victory there. It was especially pleasing as some drunkard pushed a broken dressing room door off its hinges on to my head about half an hour before I walked to the ring. I had a lump under my hair the size of a golf ball and was unsure if I should box. As ever, Brendan talked me into it, but that time I was pleased he did.

Things went back to normal from there. A few wins, a few losses, the odd draw. It was as if I had never been away. Often refs were against me, I felt, and frequently I did not get decisions I deserved. There's nothing in the rules about docking points for clowning, but I know they didn't like it. Mickey Vann, an especially famous ref who officiated a few of my fights during this time, described me in his autobiography as 'the worst boxer I ever refereed'. Thanks for that, Mick. I love you, too.

Still, there were reminders of why cracks had started to appear in the paintwork. In March 1989, Brendan asked if I would do a promoter a favour. Apparently, a show in Glasgow had fallen to bits, boxers had scratched out all over the place and they were short of fights. The request was to fight a former opponent of mine called George Bagrie again. I had knocked him out in the second round about five months earlier, but this time they had a special arrangement in mind. The promoter did not want an early knockout as he wanted to fill time, so I was to make it look good, go the distance, and help pad out the card. The money was decent, so I agreed to do it as long as Bagrie knew the craic as well.

'Course he does, Glen,' Brendan assured me. 'He's helping out the promoter, just like you are. We're all in it together.'

'Fine.'

Once I got in there, I went through the motions to begin with, but could not help but notice that George became more ambitious in the second. He started coming forward with intent, putting weight behind his punches. My suspicions were raised.

'He does know the score, doesn't he, Brendan?' I asked on my stool before the third.

'Yeah, yeah, definitely. Just jab and move and keep out of his way. It'll be fine.'

In the fourth, Bagrie got steadily more aggressive and by the fifth had started winging massive rights at me, all the way from

BEYOND GOOD AND EVIL

his boots. The kid was clearly trying to knock me out. Actions speak louder than words and it was apparent by then that he had no idea what had been arranged between Brendan and the promoter. Anger grew inside me. I was being taken for a ride. Brendan was using me. Not only that, but he was putting me in danger. Why should I have to go soft against an opponent trying to take my head off? So, I turned the tide, stuck it on him and forced a stoppage in the sixth.

As might be expected, Brendan and I had a set-to afterwards.

'I can't believe you tried to do that to me,' I told him. As usual, Brendan talked his way out of it.

By this time, a lot of things had gone on and I think our relationship was much more of a standard arrangement between a fighter and their manager. I had grown up and was no longer the young lad who idolised this charismatic Irish father figure. I saw him in adult terms, and as with any realistic appraisal of another human being, some of what I saw was negative.

For his part, I don't think Brendan ever fully forgave me for working with Herol when he left him and had long ago reached the end of his tether with my lack of commitment. In addition to all of that, his stable had grown so much since I first joined the gym and his priorities were now firmly with some of the newer lads. That's the way it goes, I guess. Everything changes with time, right? And some things fall apart.

10

BY THE time 1990 rolled around, there appeared little chance of me ever achieving my great redemption as a boxer. I occupied a little niche and was known to be erratic. A guy who could give anyone a battle on my day, but also someone who could not be relied on to turn in a good performance. My New Year's resolution, as usual, was to train hard and give it all a proper go. Also as usual, I didn't do it.

At the end of January, I was booked in for another fight at Sheffield City Hall on a big night for our gym. The new kid on the block, Johnny Nelson, was challenging the Puerto Rican champion Carlos De León for the WBC cruiserweight world title. Everyone had always assumed Herol would be Brendan's first world title winner, but Nelson had a chance to jump the queue. A terrific physical specimen, with great natural attributes, Johnny was reckoned to have a decent chance against a solid but pedestrian champion.

My fight was a stinker and I lost on points to a kid called Billy Couzens. As usual, I was poorly prepared and just couldn't get myself going. Disappointing as that was, especially for my usual crowd of ticket buyers, it was nothing compared to the main event. What a night for Brendan's gym it turned out to be.

In a strange way, Nelson's fight took the pressure off me because it was so unspeakably bad. Even now, people who were there, or watched on television recall it as the worst boxing match they have ever seen.

Whether it was the occasion, or inexperience, or something else in his head, I don't know, but Johnny completely froze. He turned in a safety-first, timid performance that looked almost pathetic. He made no real attempt to engage with De León and stayed out of range, occasionally pawing a jab which never connected. Everyone kept waiting for the fight to get going, but it never did.

By the end of the 12 rounds, only a handful of punches had landed, and De León kept his belt pretty much by default. The broadcast and commentary team were utterly scathing. There was unrest in the crowd and police had to take people away who were angry at the waste of their time and money. The whole thing was deeply embarrassing for Johnny, embarrassing for Brendan, and in some ways embarrassing for all of us at St Thomas'.

I stayed away from the gym for quite a while after that show. There were lots of repercussions. Hate mail, negative press, angry phone calls. St Thomas' was not a nice place to be. Brendan said someone had even sent a white feather in an envelope addressed to Johnny, the symbol of a coward. For any boxer, that's one of the worst things you can be called.

Of course, I had some sympathy for Nelson, but in truth a large part of me felt he deserved the reaction he got. He had been given a huge opportunity, one that could potentially change his life and had allowed it to pass him by in such an abject way. The least he could have done is make a fight of it. The worst potential outcome would have been him getting knocked out, and you simply cannot go into a boxing ring, especially for a world title, afraid of that possibility.

Momentum was building though, and the end of that year saw another world title fight in our camp. After losing narrowly to Kalambay, Herol had picked up a couple of wins then fought the Jamaican Mike McCallum for the vacant WBA world title, at the end of 1989. He boxed well and lost on a narrow, split decision, which many people disagreed with. By November 1990, and following another couple of impressive victories, he was back in the world title mix.

This time, he was lined up to face the Virgin Islander Julian Jackson for the vacant WBC belt. Jackson was generally viewed as quite a limited fighter, but one who possessed lethal power. He only needed to catch you once.

The fight has since gone down in boxing folklore and is still a very popularly viewed video on YouTube. Herol boxed

Jackson's ears off for three rounds. He was masterful. One of the champion's eyes closed and the ref told Jackson at the end of the third that the damage was so bad, that he would only give him one more round, then pull him out.

That meant all Herol had to do was stay out of the way for three minutes and he would finally achieve his destiny. Again, he came out boxing beautifully, all rhythm and balance and movement. With only a minute or so left until the bell, Herol backed Jackson into a corner. Rather than do the sensible thing and retreat to kill time, Herol wanted to win like a champion. Jackson looked ready for the taking, so he came forward to apply more pressure and walked on to an unbelievably savage right hook. Bomber did not feel a thing. He was asleep before he hit the canvas.

Back at home, afterwards, this put another massive downer on the gym atmosphere. Would Brendan ever have a world champion? Bomber was so influential in that place and here he was, a super-talented guy, a pure natural who did everything right. He trained hard, ran every morning, and still couldn't win.

Despite that, on a personal level, I went on a little winning streak around this time, picking up four victories on the bounce during 1990 and 1991. I turned 30 during this time and was perhaps beginning to grow up a bit. It was also the first point in my life when boxing's darkest side reared up in front of me.

I think everybody who gets in the ring, even if it's just for a spar, knows that boxing is a dangerous sport. As soon as you start punching and being punched in the head, the possibility of serious injury is there. Most fighters don't dwell on this, but of course they are aware of it, because like everything in life, boxing is a trade-off. If the sport gives you enough positives to live with the dangers, you might be a boxer. If that level of physical risk is just too much for you, you won't.

In February 1991, I found myself on a big show at the Brighton Conference Centre, on the undercard of Chris Eubank defending his WBO world middleweight title against the Canadian, Dan Sherry. I was boxing one of Barry Hearn's young prospects, Neil Foran, and I think Barry and his team thought I would be a good work-out for this young, unbeaten kid. They were wrong.

I was on song that night and put Foran down in the first. By round two, I went into showboat mode. It was one of those nights when everything clicked. My right hands couldn't miss, and halfway through the round I caught him with a lovely right-left combo. The kid was gone, and there was no need for the referee to count.

I don't know why I did it, but I just stood over Foran and raised my hands in the air. The referee pushed me away and sent me back to my corner.

As I stood in the corner and watched Foran laid on the canvas, my sense of triumph ebbed away. The kid was not moving at all. His team surrounded him, the ringside doctor got involved and an atmosphere of concern developed. I got a feeling in my chest, which I suppose was dread. It became suffocating. I looked anxiously from side to side. How was this going to end? It seemed to go on for a very long time, until at last, he sat up. Phew.

I had a couple of fights abroad after that, one in Italy against a tough Nigerian and another in France, before an evening came along which affected me enormously.

I was still living at 8 Valentine Crescent, the council house I'd lived in since 1982. It was the first house I ever owned and the house I moved into when I got married.

I had managed to make the house a nice place with the help of friends by begging, stealing and borrowing (mainly stealing). I was building an extension to the kitchen when I got one of my regular calls from Brendan. I was sitting on the roof. My girlfriend passed the phone up to me.

'Glen, Glen, I've got yous a fight.'

I couldn't help but smile, although by this time, I was wise to the business. I stopped asking where and when by then. 'How much will I take home?'

I had learned, the hard way, not to bother asking what the purse was. Once all the deductions – manager's fees, trainer's fees, etc – came out, you always ended up with far less. Brendan told me the money. It was good.

'It's in London,' Brendan said. 'On the undercard of the Eubank v Watson fight.'

The Chris Eubank and Michael Watson rematch was the hottest ticket in British boxing at the time. The first fight had ended in a controversial points win for Eubank and their second bout was set to take place at White Hart Lane stadium, the ground of Tottenham Hotspur Football Club.

'Brendan,' I said.

'Yes, Glen.'

'That show's tomorrow night.'

'I know, I know,' he replied. 'But the money's good, right?'

I was never one to turn down a payday too often. I had not been near the gym for ages, but that was my standard way of working by then.

My fight and the build-up to it turned out to be a great experience. When we arrived at the ground, the ring was just being erected and all the TV people were running around. I had never boxed on such a big event before and once the place started to fill up, it looked fantastic. I was genuinely excited beforehand.

Bearing in mind that it was my 59th professional bout and I was pretty world-weary and cynical about it all by then, that was unusual.

I got ready in the dressing room and when the runner called me, I walked up the tunnel to the edge of the football pitch and looked out over to the ring in the middle of the field. There was capacity for 20,000 people there and the seats were already filling up nicely. It was a stirring sight.

The ring-walk was so long it actually tired my legs a bit before starting. I boxed the Irishman Eamon Loughran, who was an undefeated 14-fight prospect at the time. Loughran was a very accomplished boxer but had not fought anyone like me. I knew I was up against it, so stood on his toes, called him names. I even hit him in the balls, anything I could think of to throw him off his game.

I gave a decent account of myself and lost on points but Loughran would be a world champion within five years so it was pretty creditable.

I went back to the changing room, got dressed and stood by the side of the arena to watch the main fight. By the time Watson and Eubank got in the ring, the atmosphere was unbelievable. I watched the action unfold in what was an incredible fight until Watson was stopped at the beginning of round 12. None of us knew how serious his injuries were, but it was clear from where I stood that chaos was unfolding. The ring filled with people and officials rang around panicking. At last, Watson was put on a stretcher and carried right past where I stood. I had a camera with me and managed to get a picture of him.

As the night went on and after he was rushed to hospital, we learned more about the damage he had suffered. No one knew if he would live or die.

Seeing what happened to Michael Watson drained some of my remaining motivation. Not that I would have admitted it publicly, but it preyed on my mind.

Watson's recovery was in the news constantly. Things sounded pretty grim. He was in a coma for 40 days, then spent about eight months unable to move, hear or talk, until he started to regain some motor function. What really got me, was that the guy was a model pro. He was super fit, very dedicated and also an excellent fighter. If something like that could happen to him, what did it mean for a guy like me, who took most of his fights without having trained?

Boxing had been my focus throughout my adult life. In one sense the sport could even be described as my saviour, but the Michael Watson situation was the first time I began to question it a little bit. It's not easy to come up with answers when something like that happens.

I had one more fight in 1991, out in Switzerland just before Christmas, which was a shitty experience all round. The hotel was shitty, the people were shitty, and my performance was shitty. I just could not wait to get out of there and return home.

There's a common saying in boxing that the fighter is the last to know it's over. But I disagree. The fighter is the first to know it's over, but maybe the last to admit it to himself.

I already had that feeling.

Back home, over Christmas, I didn't talk about it, but went over and over the whole thing in my mind. In the past I had always found a reason to box again. The money was a big factor, but also the fact that I loved to fight. This time, I could not think of a reason to continue fighting, so once again, I started to wonder what I could do with the rest of my life.

At 31, I may have been getting old in boxing terms, certainly for a lightweight in that era, but was still a young man in the eyes of society. The future stretched ahead of me like a great ocean. I could either find a way to navigate it, or just jump in and drown.

To me, boxing was still the greatest sport in the world. It was the only one that had ever grabbed me. I was never one for football or cricket. In boxing you find pure one-on-one confrontation you never really get anywhere else, but the sport and the business side of it do not really match up. It's very hard to set yourself up for when you retire.

For a start, the adrenaline of competition is addictive. Once you get used to walking out under those lights and doing battle, even if it's just at small hall events, it's not easy to leave that behind and settle for a regular routine. One day, you're literally risking your life, living by your wits, living in the moment, the next you're driving a van, working in a factory or washing dishes. It's a tough one.

Added to that is the hard truth that only a tiny minority of boxers make enough money to live comfortably for the rest of their lives. Most retire broke and have to face a feeling of uselessness. When you no longer do the only thing you were ever good at, what are you left with? Suddenly you're just a bloke with lumpy hands, cauliflower ears, scarred eyebrows and probably a bit of brain damage, wandering around in the normal world like a freak.

The worst part about stopping fighting is that the instinct to fight is ingrained, and never leaves you. Fighters are destroyers. If they're not allowed to try to destroy others anymore, they can end up destroying themselves.

11

AT THE start of 1992, I bit the bullet and got a job working on doors in Sheffield city centre again. I found it embarrassing. Despite being quite well known as a local boxer, I was penniless, earning meagre wages and dealing with pricks who couldn't fight if their lives depended on it.

I saw no future in door-work and racked my brains. What other legitimate channels were there for me to make money?

One of my mates asked if I wanted to help him install UPVC windows. I did that for a while, but it bored me. So, I packed it in and decided to go to college.

The kid who left school at 16 without a single qualification managed to get a City & Guilds in construction but did not enjoy it. I was older than some of the teachers and felt a right idiot. So, I did what so many retired boxers do, I drifted back to the gym.

I told myself I was only returning for the social side of things. I went back to working doors again, with the same attitude I always had – I would wait to see what else would come up. Getting back in the gym and seeing the lads gave me such a lift. It made me feel myself again. Naturally, I began to spar. It was the only aspect of training I had ever liked. Naseem Hamed was an adult by then and at the outset of his career. The gym had such a buzz. I had not spoken much with Brendan. We acknowledged each other with looks instead, but I had been back a month or so, when my phone rang.

'Glen, Glen, I've got yous a fight.'

'I bet you have.'

'It's in Stoke, the kid's not up to much. It'll be easy, just do your thing, mess him about, you'll be fine.'

Of course, I took it. For once, Brendan's description was accurate. My opponent, Mark Pain, outweighed me by nearly a stone, which had not been mentioned, but wasn't too much of a challenge. I just ran around sticking my jab out for six rounds and beat him on points.

With that one under my belt, everything immediately went back to what I thought of as 'normal'. We are all creatures of habit, aren't we? I did not go to the gym to train, just to see my mates, spar and have a laugh. I told Brendan to call when he had a fight for me, then I would start training seriously. I'm sure by this point he didn't believe me, and I don't think I really believed it myself, but it felt like I was supposed to say it, so I did.

So, 1993 began the way so many of the previous 14 years had. I was still a professional boxer, still managed and promoted

BEYOND GOOD AND EVIL

by Brendan, and still in this strange state of feeling a deep affinity for boxing, for the soul of the sport, but unable to commit to it properly. I'm sure there's a profound meaning in that, somewhere.

I told my old friends in Miami that I was boxing again, and they invited me over to train with them. In the meantime, Brendan got me a fight in Manchester against Tony Ekubia. Ekubia was a good fighter, who had been British and Commonwealth welterweight champion and the show was to be televised on Eurosport, which meant a slightly higher purse. I did okay but ran out of steam and got stopped in the sixth. As I so often did, I messed Ekubia around as much as possible and I think the stoppage resulted from the ref, Ron Hackett, getting fed up with me as much as anything else. Ron reffed a number of my fights and was quite open about how much I frustrated him.

I had another soon after that, a second-round KO win over a guy called Mike Phillips in Stoke. With the money from that one in the bank, I had enough to travel to America.

Just before I flew out, I was approached by a new, local promoter called Dennis Hobson. The Hobson family were well known around Sheffield and Dennis ran his own gym, which at that time was still quite a low-key affair and nothing compared to the stable Brendan had built. Dennis asked if I would fight on a show he was staging at the Octagon Centre and I told him I would. Brendan and I only worked on a handshake so there did not seem any harm in me getting work through someone else.

I flew to Miami, trained in Angelo Dundee's place again as I had several times before, and forgot all about it. Then, the day after I got home, I went to see Brendan. I had spent a lot of money while I was away, was skint, of course, and needed a fight as soon as possible. That was music to Brendan's ears.

What was strange was that as I was leaving the gym, he stopped me.

'Glen, one more thing. I need you to come to me house to sign a new contract.'

I asked why and he said he was getting all his fighters to sign new contracts and it needed to happen now and blah blah. As usual, Brendan managed to persuade me.

So, we walked over to his house, across from the gym and signed this contract, with Alma, Brendan's wife, acting as a witness. I found the whole episode weird and formal but accepted it as one of Brendan's quirky moments. Anyone who spent any time with him quickly became used to those.

The next day, it all began to make a little more sense. I got a phone call to say someone had seen a poster of me in the Wicker, so I drove there for a look. 'Dennis Hobson promotions presents ...'

It was pleasing to see a big poster with my name topping the bill in my hometown, so I went home, phoned Dennis and thanked him for wanting to promote me. Dennis also said he wanted to be my manager. He had phoned the BBBoC while I was in America and had been told I was a free agent, which technically I had been. He said he really enjoyed my boxing style, wanted to look after me and see what we could achieve together.

You didn't have to be a genius to figure out that Brendan must have somehow caught wind of this. As soon as he found out someone else wanted to promote me and invest in me, he protected his assets and tied me down. I got straight on the phone to Brendan and told him what I thought. Why couldn't he just have been honest about what was going on? But Brendan had a way of turning things around and soon convinced me it was all for the best. I think it's called reverse psychology.

By that time, I was 33 years old and when I put the phone down, could not banish a sort of sinking feeling. Perhaps Dennis Hobson had just offered my last chance to really do something in the sport. I could have finished my career headlining hometown shows, maybe fought for the Central Area title again, or even the English title. Maybe had a bit of glory.

I also felt like I had messed Dennis around and to compound that, as we all knew he would, Brendan started showing off. On the night of the show, the old goat had to be centre stage, even though I was top of the bill.

As soon as we got to the venue, Brendan started kicking off because the referee for my fight was none other than Ron Hackett again.

'If Ron Hackett is the referee, then Glyn Rhodes ain't fighting,' he shouted.

'Brendan, what are you on about?' I said in his ear. 'I've sold loads of tickets, so I'm fighting. I don't care who the referee is.'

Dennis came to see what all the fuss was about and asked Brendan to calm down and stop causing trouble. So, of course Brendan turned on him and launched into a big rant.

'What's this to you? Glyn Rhodes is my boxer. I'll have you know he's just signed a new contract. I take care of all his affairs and always have done.' He went on and on.

Nonetheless, he got his way, as he tended to, and the referee was changed to Tony Green, who also happened to be Brendan's very good friend. I won on points in a poor, scrappy fight, despite suffering a cut eye from a clash of heads.

Then something truly weird happened. As the referee raised my hand, the crowd, my hometown crowd, started booing the result. I stood there, looking out over the arena with Sheffield people booing me. It was a horrible feeling. I knew I had not boxed well but didn't think I deserved that.

My cut eye was stitched, then I went out to meet my mates, but was not happy at all. The aftermath of the fight left me feeling sick and I ended up going home early, stewing in my own juices again. Boxing had given me lots of highlights, but in the last few years, the lows seemed to be becoming more frequent.

Brendan phoned me two days later. He knew I had been shaken by events at the Octagon show, so I naively thought he might be calling to see how I was. No chance.

'Glen, Glen, I've got yous a fight.'

'Okay. How much?'

He wanted me to box in London against the Southern Area welterweight champion, Gary Logan, who had 21 wins from 22 fights. The fight date was 23 May, only ten days after my last contest.

'What about my cut eye, I only had the stitches out a couple of days ago?' I asked.

'Don't worry about it,' Brendan said. 'You'll be fine. You're too experienced for him. Just fiddle him around, keep him guessing. This kid won't get near you.'

I accepted, predictably. Equally predictably, it turned into an awful night for me. Emotionally, I don't think I was ready. I was still wounded from the Octagon show. Gary Logan was no mug and my cut reopened in the first round. As I got off my stool to start the second, I knew I was done. I did not want to do this anymore.

I was almost 34 years old and had 65 professional fights behind me. I had won 33, lost 27 and drawn 5 times when I should have won. I had fought eight times abroad and never got a result. I had fought five kids who would go on to be British champions, two French champions, two Commonwealth champions, a European champion and one who went on to be world champion. I had bone grafts on my hands and had broken my nose multiple times. I even broke my ankle once. I had more stitches in my face than Frankenstein's monster and had suffered a fractured cheekbone.

I had earned quite a lot of money from boxing but saved none of it. All this went through my head in a couple of seconds. I looked out at the London crowd baying for my blood and thought, 'nope'.

Gary Logan stopped me in the next round.

12

IT WAS my third retirement, but I also knew this one was real – 34 was old for a lightweight in the early nineties. Some of my later fights were against welters, and I did not want to carry on for the sake of it, going up weight class by weight class and being used as a punchbag for up-and-comers. That's the way things were probably heading if I kept at it.

I went to sign on as unemployed, a chastening experience. At the dole office, there would nearly always be someone there who knew who I was and would ask how things were going. 'When are you boxing again?' I got asked that all the time. I made up every excuse possible, but never said that I had retired. I just found it hard to say.

I started working back on the doors, but this time even that felt different. Before there had always been the thought of a fight to look forward to. Plus, door-work was not well paid, and I was used to having a bit more in my pocket.

I got involved in some things I would never have done if I had still been boxing. I always seemed to get approached by people with dodgy schemes. For a while, I was collecting money on behalf of some local characters. A few quid for this, a few quid for that, I was the stereotypical retired boxer, mooching about with few prospects.

A few months into my new, directionless life, I was walking along Langsett Road, where some signs caught my eye. 'Impact Gym – opening soon!' The building behind them looked like it was being renovated. I walked in, just to see what was going on.

The place looked like a building site, still only half-finished. I asked a guy near the door who was in charge and was introduced to a thick-set man called Steve Baxendale. He owned a nightclub in the centre of Sheffield called Rebels, a heavy rock club and was a bit of a character around the city.

I casually asked Steve who would be teaching boxing in the new gym. He told me a coach called Andy Marlow was doing the kickboxing, but they did not have a boxing trainer yet.

'Do you fancy it?' he asked.

This was an interesting turn of events. I had never really thought about becoming a trainer and always assumed that once I retired from the ring, I would walk away from the sport altogether. I needed options, though, and this was something I could have a go at. Best of all, it was legal.

I felt the need for some advice and made the mistake of going to St Thomas' to speak to Brendan about it.

'Don't think it'll work for you, Glen', he said. 'You need the right personality, a bit of patience and a lot of passion to train youngsters. Plus, let's be honest, you're a fucking loose cannon.'

His tone sounded a little bitter. I felt that now I was no longer with him, and he wasn't making money from me, he didn't care what I did. Despite his poor appraisal of my prospects, I shook hands with Brendan and thanked him for all he had done for me. At the same time, he helped me decide to give the trainer job a go. Something inside me wanted to prove him wrong. I'm not just a *tick bastard*, I thought. There's more to me than that.

It seemed a lifetime ago since I first walked into St Thomas' in 1976. Boxing had changed the course of my life, for the better, and regardless of what had happened after that, most of that was down to him. Whatever bad feelings we may have had toward each other, I wanted him to know that I appreciated that. As usual, he didn't seem fussed, bid me goodbye and we parted ways.

Over the next month or so, I helped Steve finish setting the interior of the building up, until we had a very stylish, modern-looking gym with top-notch facilities. It was a world away from Brendan in his church hall.

Once Impact opened, crowds came straight away. I loved it. I was living on my own at the time, and didn't have much to go home for, so was in the gym all day until late at night.

Steve then asked me if I wanted a job working on the door of his nightclub, too. So, I began doing that at weekends.

I would be in the gym all day, then on Thursday, Friday and Saturday I was at Rebels. I would start at 11pm and work until 2.30am. I'd go for something to eat and head home to sleep all day.

It was an easy job and there was very little trouble. My only negative experience was that my drink got spiked a couple of times and I ended up tripping out, which I did not enjoy at all. I never found out who did it and whoever it was certainly never had the courage to own up. I was an experienced doorman by then and even though I wasn't a big bloke, I could handle most situations. My years of boxing gave me sharp instincts and when you're dealing with drunkards, it's not hard to get the better of them.

Before long, Herol started appearing in the gym, and it was great having him around. He had retired too after losing to Sumbu Kalambay again and then getting stopped by a guy called Frank Grant in a British title fight. Age had caught up with him too, sadly.

I booked yet another little holiday to Miami and asked Bomber to cover for me while I was away. This proved to be a bit of poor judgement, on my part.

When I got back to England, Steve said he thought it would be a good idea if Herol and I managed the boxing together from then on. What he really meant was that while I was in Miami, Herol did such a great job that he had decided to split my wages between the two of us.

It was also clear to me that from a marketing point of view, Steve thought it was better to have Herol 'Bomber' Graham, golden boy and former British, European and Commonwealth champion, working in the gym, rather than Glyn Rhodes. It would look much better on posters and help attract more customers, in his mind.

It felt like a betrayal, but I swallowed it. I had helped Herol out with a bit of work and gone over and above with Steve in getting the gym up and running, and my reward was to lose my job. Bomber was apologetic when I saw him, saying it was all Steve's idea, but if I am honest, they both pissed me off with how they behaved.

It was then, for the first time, I started to formulate plans to start my own gym. I had no clue how to do it but knew I could not continue to work for Steve Baxendale, alongside Herol. The job-share did not work for me, professionally or financially.

If I was my own boss, I understood that would mean shouldering a level of risk, but I knew it would also mean eliminating the possibility of being backstabbed by my employer. All I had to do was find some suitable premises and take it from there.

I dealt with this new ambition on a need-to-know basis and barely mentioned it to anyone. One of the people I did raise it with was an old friend of mine called Martin, who ran a bodybuilding gym in another part of town. He was very encouraging and introduced me to a friend of his named Mick, who happened to be a big boxing fan and knew who I was. Mick ran a waste disposal business on the Wybourn council estate and the premises he owned was over two storeys, with his office downstairs. The upper floor was not really in use and after a couple of conversations it was decided I could use it for my gym.

Fuelled by a sense of excitement, I started work straight away. Darren Wright, my best friend since childhood helped me out, and between us we got the place looking pretty good. Within a month or two, it was ready.

At that point, I told Herol and everyone else at Impact that I was leaving. It seemed the only person surprised to hear this was Herol, although splitting with Steve also meant I stopped working the door at Rebels. This raised the stakes a little bit. As my new venture got underway, I had no other income. If the gym flopped, I would be back at the Job Centre or collecting money for gangsters before long.

Sometimes, I guess, there's magic in boldness. Things seemed to work from the get-go. Large numbers of customers left Impact to come to train at my new place. In fact, Impact began to struggle within a few months and Steve sold it. After that, Herol came to ask if he could work with me at my gym. I didn't want any hard feeling between us, so took him on.

Darren and I kept it all ticking along, but despite my long professional career, neither of us had any qualifications. To formalise things, we needed to go on a four-day course organised by the Amateur Boxing Association.

This was a strange experience as the people running the course all seemed like well-meaning, PE teacher types but did not really know what they were on about. They also gave the impression of being quite anti-professional boxing. Any mention of it and they immediately became flustered.

Some of them were coaches for the England team, but it's easy to train a kid who is already good enough to get picked for England. It's some other trainer who has spent hours teaching the boxer his left foot from his right, how to jab and move his feet. What you don't want to see is some prick in a black blazer and a badge taking all the credit and thinking they are more important than the fighter.

I had never been the type of guy to have much time for boxing officials. I had heard the way they spoke to kids when they were getting weighed in. I had even seen them sitting with a pint of beer and smoking, talking to the kids like dogs. These are nervous youngsters, in some cases having their first bout. It is a side of the game I have always hated.

At one point, near the end of the course, Darren and I were asked to come into the centre of the hall, to demonstrate a left hand to the body. So, I jabbed Darren's body and the beer-bellied instructor said, 'No, no, no, that's not how you do it.'

I could not believe what I was hearing. I had 30 amateur and 65 pro fights behind me and this guy who had learned boxing from a manual was telling me how to throw a punch.

'Okay then,' I replied. 'How would you throw a left hand to the body?'

He stepped forward and stood there like he had a pole up his arse.

'This is how you do it,' he said proudly, performing a strange kind of squat. 'Bend your knees, then once you're down, push out the left hand.'

He looked absolutely ridiculous, like something out of a cartoon. I feinted a big right in his direction, just to prove a point and he lost balance and fell over. Everyone in the hall cracked up laughing. Of course, the instructor was fuming, as I had undermined his authority.

Darren and I kept our heads down after that, received our little ABA badges to sew on our tracksuits and a couple of certificates we could put on the gym wall, to say we were fully qualified boxing coaches. I was still not totally sure what to do for the rest of my life, but that meant I could be in this for the long haul.

13

AN IMMEDIATE effect of the new accreditation was that Darren and I were allowed to work the corners at shows. This stepped the gym up a level, and we had a number of kids applying for their amateur cards, then getting out and competing. This all seemed to happen very quickly.

Things soon took an even more serious turn, though. Herol turned up one day with a fighter who had been a stablemate of his while he was managed by Barney Eastwood. Herol said he was looking for a gym.

Richie Wenton was an extremely solid professional, with a 16-fight record and 15 wins to his name. He buzzed about in the gym, a stereotypical, livewire Scouser in a tracksuit, talking at a hundred miles an hour.

Richie was from a famous boxing family in Liverpool, had split with his previous trainer and asked if I would train him for an upcoming fight. He was set to box Des Gargano, a journeyman with a losing record, but someone who was known to be very tough and potentially a tricky opponent if in the wrong mood. The whole thing was a strange affair as Richie was also co-promoter of the show, alongside another pro called Carl Bailey. It was one of those 'why not?' moments and I agreed to train him. My gym had only been open about half a year and I already had my first pro.

For some reason which I have never fully fathomed, Richie and Carl chose to host their maiden boxing event in a tiny, one-horse town called Cullompton in Devon. If you made a top ten list of weirdest places to hold a boxing show in the UK, it would have to be near the top. It was in the middle of nowhere and had a population of about 6,000 people.

Richie also wanted his training camp based down there as he needed to organise the show while preparing for his fight. I was due to stay with Richie at a house he had arranged, so set off on the long train journey to Devon, on the basis that Richie would meet me at the station.

On arrival, I was the only one to disembark. The station was deserted, so I sat on my suitcase and waited. As my eyes grew accustomed to the dark, I could see rabbits in the field across the train tracks. Before long, paranoia kicked in and I started thinking I could see other things in the gloom. Shadowy shapes, weird lights. An owl hooted nearby. It was like the opening scene of a horror movie.

After a couple of hours of going slowly insane, I saw the headlights of a car in the distance, driving towards the station.

It was hurtling down the narrow country road, swerving around corners and throwing up dust in its wake.

The car screeched to a stop beside me, and Richie jumped out.

'All right, Glyn, how are ya, mate?' he said, in his squeaky Scouse voice.

'Where the fuck have you been? I've been sat here for hours,' I chided.

'Ah, don't worry about it, Glyn. I fell asleep while I was watching the telly.'

This was obviously a wonderful start to our professional relationship.

'If you hadn't woken up, I'd have still been here in the fucking morning,' I said, still annoyed.

We got into the car, and Richie screeched the wheels as we drove off. When we arrived at his house, he took me upstairs into a box room with an unmade bed and nothing else.

'Is this all right for ya, mate?' he asked.

'Sheets, pillows, anything like that?'

He left the room and came back with a quilt. 'Is this all right for ya, mate?' he said again.

I thought there was no way I was going to last with this nutcase. He had a reputation for going through trainers one after the other and I was beginning to see why. While in Devon, we trained in a little gym in a village called Bideford. They were not used to meeting professional sportspeople down there and treated Richie like a celebrity, which he absolutely loved.

As the show neared, Herol came down too, with his British title belt. The people of Cullompton fussed over him too and he thrived on the attention, just like Richie.

The day of the show rolled around, and we were all relaxing in Richie's house when the phone rang. Carl Bailey's opponent had pulled out. This was a major blow to the viability of the show and panic ensued, so I took Richie to one side and made a suggestion.

'Why don't you offer Herol a few quid to do a boxing exhibition? The people here would love to watch Herol doing his stuff.'

I knew Herol was skint, since his retirement, and I knew if they offered him some money, he would do it.

'Great idea!' Richie said. 'But who can he box?'

The idea was thrown open to the room, to see if anyone had any suggestions. Eyes kept turning to me.

'You could do it couldn't ya, mate?' Richie asked.

'Don't be stupid. I couldn't live with Herol when I was boxing, never mind now.'

Then Herol chipped in. By this point he was fully on board and looking forward to his payday.

'Come on, Glyn. It'll be okay. We'll look after each other. We've sparred hundreds of rounds over the years.'

I took a lot of convincing, but in the end, I agreed to do it for £100. Herol was getting £200 and I could not understand why I was getting paid less when I was the one who needed danger money.

As soon as the exhibition was announced, the locals went mad. Herol was signing autographs and surrounded whenever he moved. It was like he was Muhammad Ali.

We borrowed some boxing gear for me to wear and I climbed between the ropes wearily. Once the bell rang though, the experience of it all was disconcerting. It seemed alien. I used to be so at home in the ring, but not anymore. Every cell in my brain was screaming, 'What the fuck are you doing?'

Herol and I had made some plans in the changing room as to how we would play it. The idea was that I would just make Herol look good, follow him around and let him do his stuff. The plan lasted about 30 seconds.

Herol obviously enjoyed shaking the rust off, instincts kicked in, and he switched back into fight mode. He stuck out his right glove as a range finder, then hammered me to the body with a left uppercut. It took all the breath out of me.

I grabbed hold of him, got in his ear and said, 'What're you doing, you fucking idiot?'

Herol pushed me off, then started moving around the ring again. It was a taste of things to come. He was determined to make me look silly.

In the second, Herol pulled the same move again, only this time I went down. I felt like I had been hit by a truck. Herol was about 13 stone at the time. I was about ten and a half.

The referee started counting over me, so I got up and shouted at him, 'It's only an exhibition you know!' Everyone was laughing, Herol included. I'm sure they thought I was enjoying myself too, but I wasn't.

I had a massive go at Herol in the ring, in front of everyone, and the crowd just laughed harder like it was all part of the act.

After it was all over, Herol signed autographs, had his picture taken and generally got treated like royalty, while I just went back to the changing room to sort Richie out. That's how it goes when you're playing second fiddle. Even in retirement, I was still just Herol's supporting act.

Richie's fight was by no means a classic. He won on points against a very durable opponent but didn't look good. My feeling was that he had been distracted. I didn't think it was the best idea for him to box on the show as well as promote it and told him so.

After our Devon adventure and perhaps against my better judgement, I continued working with Richie Wenton. Five months after that strange Cullompton show, Richie was scheduled to box for the newly introduced British super-bantamweight title at the York Hall in Bethnal Green, London.

He was going to be up against a tough kid called Bradley Stone, but all of us were excited about it. Our gym was still a fledgling venture, really, and if we had a British champion among our ranks, it would make a little statement.

As before, it was a nightmare trying to train Richie. He was always bouncing around here and there, like a Tasmanian devil, and it was difficult to get him to focus on one thing at a time. Herol had him living at his house, so he could monitor his bedtimes and take him out for runs. He even cooked Richie's meals.

It was funny to the rest of us, as day by day you could see the toll that living with Richie took on Herol. Every time he turned up at the gym, he looked a little more frazzled. With a British title to be gained, though, we all hoped it would be worth it.

14

A WEEK before the big fight, my mate Paul 'Silky' Jones, a top light-middleweight, who I had known since training at Brendan's together as youngsters, asked if I would do him a favour. A friend of his needed someone to work the door of an Indian restaurant that had been having regular trouble with drunken louts late at night. I told Paul that I was happy to help.

Richie came up too, out of boredom more than anything else, and the two of us sat by the door and talked boxing. The place was packed, but for the first part of the evening everything was quiet and there was nothing for us to do.

Around 10pm, a table of four blokes behind us started getting a little loud. It was all just beery nonsense but made other customers feel uncomfortable, so I went over and asked them, very politely, to keep the noise down. As I walked away, one of them said something back. I didn't hear it, but they all belly laughed. I chose not to respond but knew from experience it wouldn't end there.

A short while later, a young waiter, no more than 18 or 19 years old, brought their meals, and one of them started giving him a hard time.

'We didn't fucking order that, pal. Take it the fuck back.'

The waiter assured them they did order what he had brought them, and they all started mouthing off.

'Don't fucking try and bullshit us, you wanker. We know what we ordered. Take it back to the fucking kitchen ...' And so on. Other diners looked nervously over their shoulders. The restaurant owners gave me a look, so I rushed over, got hold of the clever twat who thought he was so tough, and told him he was leaving. He gobbed off a bit, but I pushed him to the door and kicked him out. As I did, he was telling me what he was going to do to me, that I didn't know who I was dealing with, all the usual crap I've heard before.

When I returned to the restaurant, all his mates had their heads together, scheming and plotting, but I knew if they were brave enough to do anything they would have done it by then. I approached their table.

'You can stay,' I said. 'If you'll be quiet and eat your meals. If not, you can go. What's it to be?' They all looked at each other, then stood up and said they were going. I told them to pay for their meals on their way out, which they objected to.

'Listen boys, I know you think there's three of you and only one of me, but you're wrong.' I pointed to Richie. 'There's two of us and we haven't been drinking, so make your minds up, which way do you want it?'

Sheepishly, they paid their bill, then walked towards the door. As they were leaving, one of them turned to me and said, 'You don't know who you're messing with.'

'That's funny,' I replied. 'That's just what your mate said.'

I went and sat back down with Richie and the atmosphere in the restaurant calmed.

It was how a restaurant should be. Quiet conversations, a bit of music playing, the sounds of pleasant conversation. That lasted about five minutes.

Without any warning whatsoever, the large, plate-glass window on the storefront came crashing in. Shards of glass and dust showered into the air. The suspended ceiling caved, as a van, engine roaring, shoved its way about 15 feet into the restaurant. The crazy bastards had decided to get their revenge by doing something out of a Mad Max film.

People screamed and ran everywhere. It felt like time was moving in slow motion. Once inside, the nutter in the driving seat tried to reverse, but there was so much debris on the floor that the wheels couldn't grip. They just spun and screeched on the carpet. Then he tried going forwards but couldn't do that either. I looked sideways at Richie, who had found a huge kitchen knife from somewhere and was brandishing it, as if that was going to be any good against a van.

Eventually, the nutter managed to reverse out of the building, into the middle of Chesterfield Road, did a three-point turn and sped off. All of us in the restaurant were in shock, quietly looking around, dust on our faces and clothes. The place looked like it had been hit by an airstrike.

I took it upon myself to speak to some of the customers to make sure they were okay and approached a group of women who were visibly shaken.

'Look on the bright side, ladies,' I said. 'At least you won't have to pay for your meals.' I thought a little humour might restore a sense of normality.

One of them gave me a sharp look. 'That's really not funny at a time like this,' she said. So, I pushed a plate full of dust and dirt towards her. 'You can still eat your curry if you want,' I said.

Somehow, from that starting point, we got talking. She was very pretty, with Chinese features. Her name was Hilary Wong.

Everyone did their best to help clean up the restaurant while we waited for the police to arrive. When the law came, they took statements from everyone, while emergency builders boarded up the front of the restaurant. I just sat and talked to Hilary for hours. Among other things, we discovered our birthdays were the same, 22 October.

I took Hilary home that night and pretty much fell in love with her there and then. We went on to spend the next 15 years together and have two children. She was my one true love and I suppose it's fitting in some ways that I met her in the circumstances I did. Whenever anybody asked how we met, at least we always had a decent story to tell.

Following that dramatic night at the Indian restaurant, the next week was dominated by the build-up to the biggest night of my short career as a trainer. Richie seemed in good shape physically and mentally and we all thought he could do it. The only thing that worried us was home advantage. Bradley Stone was a Londoner and would have the York Hall crowd on his side. It was the first time in a long time that I began to feel nervous as the fight approached. In my own career I had become so used to fighting on short notice that I mostly walked to the ring as if I was walking to the office. This was different somehow. Richie had trusted me to prepare him and all I could do was try to keep him focused, then hope for the best.

On the day of the fight, my friend Darren Crooks and his girlfriend drove us down to London. Richie, of course, was yammering on in the back seat and getting on everybody's nerves. I sat there rolling my eyes in silence but promised myself, again, that this was it. I would never train Richie Wenton again. The kid was such hard work.

We arrived at our hotel in London, got out of the car and suffered a major scare when Darren's girlfriend slammed the car door right on to Richie's left hand. Richie shouted in pain and Darren leapt forward to prise the door open, as we all looked on, fearing dislocations or breaks. To everyone's surprise, Richie pulled his fingers out painlessly. They were a little red and puffy but no more than that. What a reprieve.

Predictably the York Hall was packed and rowdy. I loved that old venue, as most boxing people did. It could be such a bear-pit on the right night. Even with so much at stake, Richie boxed extremely well, and I was so proud of him. His opponent Bradley Stone put up a great showing too, and from ringside I felt it was one of the best fights I had ever seen. Both fighters threw and took some great shots, but Richie was able to finish the stronger of the two and forced a stoppage in the tenth round.

So, I had my first British champion, at a time when my gym had been up and running less than a year. It was a great feeling and gave me a sense of vindication. Maybe Brendan had been wrong about me. Maybe this was the right career for me, after all?

We celebrated our win, then went into the other changing room to say well done to Bradley and his team. It takes two to make a great fight and Stone had been superb. I told him I was sure his time would come.

Then we made our way back up the M1 to Sheffield, arriving home in the early hours of the morning. I stayed in bed late into the following day but as I laid there, glued to the pillow, I could hear my phone ringing and ringing from the kitchen. Eventually, I thought I should get up.

When I listened to my messages, it seemed the phone calls were from reporters, wanting to know about the fight the night before. My phone rang again, and the caller introduced himself as being from ITV.

'Have you heard what happened last night?' he asked.

I was still half asleep. 'Yes, of course I know what happened,' I replied. 'I was there, you know.'

'So, what are your thoughts on what happened after the fight?'

A feeling of dread rose in my guts, as if I sensed what he was about to say.

'What do you mean?' I asked.

'Bradley Stone collapsed afterwards with a brain bleed. He's in hospital on a life-support machine now.'

It didn't feel real. I rubbed my eyes and asked the reporter to tell me again. He did.

I tried to process what I was being told, but it wasn't easy. Stone had seemed okay when we spoke to him in the dressing room. Soon after, Richie phoned me.

He sounded shell-shocked, his voice shaky and quiet. 'Have you heard what's happened?' he asked.

'Let's just stay calm until we find out the details.' I advised.

For the rest of that day, my phone did not stop ringing. One reporter called me, with street noises behind her, passing vehicles, the occasional siren.

I told her I could hardly hear her and asked where she was calling me from.

'I'm outside Richie Wenton's house with a camera crew,' she said. 'But Richie won't come to the door.'

I couldn't believe what I was hearing.

'You sick bastards!' I shouted. 'You're sat outside his house?'

She retained her professional manner. 'Mr Rhodes, can you tell us how Richie's feeling right now?'

'Richie Wenton is devastated,' I said. 'He's just won the British title but all we're thinking about is Bradley Stone and we hope he gets better soon.'

I drove down to my gym, only to find a TV crew waiting for me there. The whole situation was so overwhelming. They asked if they could film where Richie had been training for the title fight and I refused, saying the gym was to be closed until further notice, or until we knew Bradley Stone was okay, a decision I made on the spot.

So, I went back home only to be bombarded with further phone calls.

The story was everywhere, newspapers, radio, TV. I sat at home listening to and watching the coverage. As the Yorkshire Television news started, they announced they would be showing the gym where Richie Wenton trained and would interview a close friend of Richie's.

'Hang on,' I thought. 'I sent them away.'

The news began and sure enough, after a while, the cameras were in my gym. I was absolutely fuming, wondering who had let them in. I almost fell off my chair when Mick, the waste disposal guy from downstairs, was shown standing in the ring with his chest puffed out, saying 'Yes, this is where Richie trained blah, blah, blah.'

Mick had not even come to the fight, but was clearly enjoying his five minutes of fame, earned off the back of a very sensitive, uncertain situation. That absolutely boiled my piss.

Those days after the fight were horrible for everybody. I could not even begin to imagine how Bradley's mum and family were feeling. They must have been through hell.

It was also a terrible time for Richie. Reporters hounded him. The promoter, Frank Warren, found him somewhere to stay, just to get away from the paparazzi camping out by his door, day and night.

As his trainer, the whole situation was a big challenge for me. What can you say to a young kid who should be celebrating a British title win, but is sick with worry instead?

Two days after Richie's win, I was watching some junior contests at an amateur boxing show at Bramall Lane football ground, when I got a phone call from Richie to tell me Bradley had died. I had to get up and go outside to speak to him, but neither of us knew what to say. It was one of those moments when the world around you fades into the background. I felt awful, on a personal level. Yes, boxing is dangerous and everyone mad enough to get involved knows that, but nonetheless I had played a part in that young man's death. It was even worse for Richie, of course.

These are not easy things to square away in your mind. I wanted to call someone, but who could I call, and what was I going to say to them? In the tried and trusted method of men throughout the centuries, Richie and I both swallowed our guilt and grief, bottling them up, trying our best to forget them. We had no other way to cope.

15

WE TRIED to get back to some sort of normality in the gym, but things felt wrong. Mostly, I didn't feel the same towards Mick.

All I could think about was the interview he gave on TV, pretending to be involved in the boxing set-up to get a bit of reflected glory, while a tragedy was unfolding. He looked a prick doing it and it really annoyed me.

He tried to repair the damage, coming up every now and then for some banter, but the final straw for me was when he said, 'Now Bomber Graham's training here with us, he should keep his hands up.'

I almost choked on my own tongue.

At the time, I was not happy in general. I wouldn't have used the terminology, but I think I was depressed because of what had happened to Bradley Stone. I didn't feel that I particularly wanted to stay in the game, but as usual I was faced with a lack of options. Without boxing all I had ever been was a doorman. It wasn't a tempting possibility.

So, I started thinking of moving. I thought a fresh start might help to reinvigorate me and more than anything, I wanted to get away from Mick. When he heard about this, he got stroppy and told me that if I moved out, half of my equipment was his. I asked him how he thought that was.

He was a clever bastard and said possession counts in the eyes of the law. It was his building, after all, so he had a rightful claim to the equipment inside it.

'Okay, you wanker,' I thought. 'This is how it's going to be.'

I started looking for a new place and found a great site for a gym, so started to hatch a plan to get my stuff out of Mick's place without him knowing.

I asked virtually everyone I knew with wheels if they would help me move out, especially friends who had vans. I planned the whole thing for a Saturday, as I knew Mick's staff downstairs would finish at lunchtime. The idea was to dismantle our gear during the morning, then get it all out as soon as his employees left.

We managed it, in the end, stripping the place like a bunch of locusts. My mates all stopped off at the pub and arrived the worse for wear, meaning we had a couple of accidents, including smashing one of Mick's windows, but we got the stuff out. Mission accomplished.

Of course, on Monday morning, after finding the broken window and the upper floor empty, Mick phoned me, threatening all sorts of things. I told him to fill his boots and waited for his next move. Nothing ever happened.

So, from then I was all on my own, and had rent to pay every week. I had to get my new place up and running as soon as possible. Lots of friends helped and I will be indebted to those people forever. My new location was on Carlisle Street just to the north of the city centre, in a big, old steelworks that had been converted into smaller units. I called it the Sheffield Boxing Centre or 'SBC' for short. The place was large enough to have six bags and two rings.

It was a really positive time. Old friends of mine started calling into the gym giving it a nice community feel, and back at home, Hilary moved in with me. As the trauma of the Bradley Stone fight receded further into the past, everything began to feel a little better.

Among the visitors was an old pal called Dave Davies. He was one of those people who just loved hanging around the boxing game, had loads of money, and used to be a regular visitor down at Brendan's in the old days.

Dave suggested that I should consider putting on a boxing show, which planted a seed in my mind. Thanks to his help and inspiration, my first night as a promoter of amateur boxing was scheduled for Pitsmoor Working Men's Club, on Wednesday, 1 March 1995. Dave's family ran a printing business and sorted all the tickets and posters. An old fella

I knew from my time with Brendan said he would do the matchmaking. We were all set.

Then, on the morning of the show, I got a phone call from the ABA telling me that regulations stipulated I had to have a stretcher at ringside.

'Oh, I know, of course,' I told them, then put the phone down. Where the hell was I going to get a stretcher on the day of the show?

I rang round everyone I knew to see if I could borrow a stretcher, without luck, until I phoned my pal, Darren.

'Don't worry,' he said. 'I'm working at the Northern General Hospital tarmacking the drive, I'll sort something out. Give me an hour.'

Hilary and her friend Kelsey worked the door for me, and the night overall was a great success, and absolutely packed out. The bar even ran out of beer. We went out to celebrate afterwards, with Hilary carrying the takings around in a big bag, like a bank robber. Suddenly it felt like I was going places.

From there, a kind of snowball effect kicked in. I put on some more shows, my gym became more popular, and I soon discovered that the more successful you become, the more some people won't like it.

Brendan, in particular, was bothered by me at this time. I guess I had become a competitor of his and in truth, a few kids from his gym had left and come to train with me. That's just what happens when a new gym opens, but I think Brendan took it personally.

For my part, I was always polite when I saw Brendan and would go over and shake his hand, but that changed when his new prodigy Naseem Hamed boxed the Italian, Vincenzo Belcastro at the Ponds Forge Arena for the European title.

There was a lot of hype about Naz by then, especially in Sheffield. I knew, first-hand, just how good he was and wanted to turn out to support him in his first title fight. I bought four ringside tickets, then settled myself in to watch what I was sure would be a great night of boxing.

Before the fights started, Brendan came over. I smiled. 'Brendan! How are you doing?'

'Let me see your tickets, please,' he said.

The smile slid right off my face. I was shocked and actually a little upset. He clearly thought I was trying to sneak into the ringside area. So, I pulled my tickets out of my pocket. Brendan saw them, then turned and walked away. That was it.

I struggled to believe that a man I had spent so much time with, who had influenced me so much, a man I respected and with whom I had shared fantastic experiences would treat me like that, and in front of Hilary, too. If I am honest, I was gutted. It hurt me.

People said I should just have it out with Brendan and ask him what his problem was. But I knew well enough how stubborn he could be.

During the course of the evening, I got talking to a reporter from the *Sheffield Star*, who said if I couldn't talk to Brendan, that I should write a letter and he would print it. It sounded like a decent idea, so I did. The piece came out a few days later, under the headline, 'Come on Brendan, let's end this fight'. I thought I wrote a good letter, and left it open for him to reply, but he never did. At least I tried.

By this time, I had held a trainer's licence for a while, and decided it was time to go for my manager's licence, too. The gym was buzzing, with a great bunch of amateurs and a few pros. I was loving it and feeling happy with my chosen path. More than anything, I enjoyed the atmosphere in the gym, turning up every day and having a bit of a laugh with the regulars. That side of it, the social side, makes it feel like a fantastic way to earn a living.

Before long, a familiar face reappeared in the form of Richie Wenton. He just walked in one day like a long-lost nephew, grinning from ear to ear, in one of his brightly coloured tracksuits. At first it was a bit of a shock, a reminder of darker times. I hadn't seen Richie since the Bradley Stone aftermath, when we just stopped communicating and drifted apart. I hadn't chased him, guessing that he fancied a change to take his mind off all the nastiness. I couldn't blame him for that because I had felt the same way.

There was a bit of added spice though. Since that time, Richie had disappeared for a bit then resurfaced, training at Brendan's. A month or so before he walked through my door again, he had given a big interview to the *Sheffield Star*, saying how amazing Brendan's training was, that he had never been happier and how Brendan's gym was the greatest gym going, which irked me. He must have known that there was tension between Brendan and myself, and that this would add to the public debate. One of the things you learn as a manager and trainer is that there is very little loyalty in boxing. With Richie, I was experiencing that for the first time.

'I've got a European title fight,' he said.

'Oh, you have, have you?'

'In a couple of months, in Italy.'

'Oh yeah.'

There was an awkward pause before he asked what I knew he had come to ask.

'Will you train me?' He grinned his big grin again and I rolled my eyes. I just couldn't say no to the cheeky little git. For all his faults I still thought of this kid as my fighter. My first British champion. I couldn't turn him away.

His fight was against Vincenzo Belcastro, who we had watched lose to Naz on points the previous year. Since going the distance with Hamed, a commendable feat as not many guys did in those days, Belcastro had moved up to super-bantamweight and become European champion. The contest was scheduled to take place in a town called San Benedetto, which no one in the gym had heard of.

Training with Richie was the usual palaver and predictably, it turned out to be a horrible trip. The place we stayed in was beautiful, but so remote. After you had been there for a day, you wanted to come home.

The hotel was literally up a mountain in the middle of nowhere, and there were no English newspapers, or English TV. The highlights of our day were mealtimes. Other than that, there were two choices – go for a walk, or stay where you were. So, we went for a lot of walks. The whole experience was a bit like being kept in quarantine, but with a hyperactive Scouser shadowing you, everywhere you go. All of that meant that I'm not sure Richie's head was quite in the right place on fight night. He boxed okay, but not to his best. Belcastro was a tough kid and battled away throughout. Once it went to the cards, I knew we wouldn't get a result. Italy is notorious for hometown decisions.

Once again, after returning home, I didn't hear from Richie for a while. Nonetheless, I had the feeling I would see him again before too long.

I had been back for a few days when Herol came to see me at home. He had a serious look on his face and told me he wanted to give it one last go. I listened sympathetically. Although he had achieved so much, ABA champion, then

British, Commonwealth and European titles in the pros, he had never won that world title which everyone had always believed he would.

I knew exactly where he was coming from. Boxing is a hard sport to walk away from for a lot of fighters, but for those who feel they never quite got their dues, that's especially the case. Herol was pushing 36 by then and could still look dazzling on his day. He was capable of walking in the gym and standing anyone on their head. Time was clearly against him, but he truly believed he still had a chance. I told Herol we would talk again.

That afternoon, I was in the gym as normal. It was typically busy, and I was working with a couple of kids while a host of others hit the bags. I heard the doorbell ring, and the lad monitoring the door for me shouted that there was someone outside who wanted to see me.

'Let him in then!' I yelled back.

When I turned from my pad-work to greet my visitor, I almost fainted when I saw it was Brendan. If it had been a Western film, the piano would have stopped, and everyone would have turned to look. It was that kind of moment.

'How do, Brendan?' I said. 'How can I help you?'

He said he wanted to see Herol, to get a few things straightened out. The way he spoke had an edge to it, as if he was building up to something.

I sensed a row coming.

'Listen Brendan,' I said. 'If you've got a problem with Herol, you need to sort it out with him somewhere else and not come to my gym to do it.'

He nodded slowly. 'Alright,' he said. 'Alright. Turn your music off so I can speak to all the boys you've got here.'

'What?' I was stunned. 'You can't come to my gym and start telling me and my boxers what's what.'

We exchanged a few more, increasingly tense words. Brendan's stubbornness was legendary, and I came to the conclusion that the quickest way to get rid of him was to let him speak. Otherwise, we would probably be standing there arguing for an hour.

I shouted to my door monitor to turn the music off.

'Okay, everyone!' I called out. 'Stop training and come and listen to Brendan.'

The gym fell quiet, and Brendan began talking. He wasn't saying much of consequence, just talking about his gym and the work he did. My kids mostly stood there disinterested. They didn't even really know who he was.

After a while, I interjected and asked Brendan what he hoped to get out of this. Most of my boxers had drifted off and gone back to hitting the bags. His lack of influence over my fighters seemed to anger him. He started shouting and I felt I had to step up.

'That's enough,' I yelled. 'Just go! And don't ever come here again.'

With that, he actually turned and went. As the door closed behind him, I felt a surge of mixed emotions. It had taken a lot of courage for me to say those words to Brendan, to stand up to him like that, but it also felt like a line had been drawn in the sand.

How sad.

16

WITHIN THE first two years at the new site, my gym became so busy that I had to look to move premises again, as I needed somewhere bigger. I found a great place in an old school on Burton Street in the Hillsborough area. It had been closed for a few years, meaning the only things you found there were pigeons and glue sniffers. We soon got rid of the glue sniffers. The pigeons stayed.

The rent was just £50 a week and the site caretaker was delighted by our arrival, as our presence meant there wasn't any more vandalism or little scumbags hanging around. It needed a lot of work, but eventually we turned it into a great facility with three rings and plenty of bags. There was so much spare space.

By the time we got everything up and running in early 1996, Herol was still bouncing about, itching to get back in the ring, and before long, I had Paul 'Silky' Jones training with me, who by that time was a former world champion. Jones had unexpectedly been lined up to challenge the American, Verno

Phillips for the WBO super-welterweight title in 1995 and even more unexpectedly, beat him, making him Sheffield's second world champion, alongside Naseem Hamed. He was then very unfortunate that purse disputes over his first defence led to him being stripped of the title, just three months after he won it. I felt for the kid. It's such a fantastic achievement to win a world title, and to have it taken away from you like that is heartbreaking. By the time he came to me, he was looking to rebuild, having just lost a British title fight against Ryan Rhodes, one of Brendan's boys.

The bottom line was that in a short space of time, my training career had really taken off. It was only four years since I had retired from the ring myself, but I had a full stable of fighters, from junior novices all the way up to established, title-winning pros. It was going better than I ever could have dreamed.

I then got a surprise phone call from the European featherweight champion, Billy Hardy, from Sunderland. He had a fight coming up against Naz who by then was the Ingle gym poster boy and held two of the four major world featherweight belts. Billy was staying in Sheffield because he was seeing a local girl and needed somewhere to train.

Even though I had never met Billy, I knew how good he was. I remembered watching him in a great fight against Orlando Canizales for the world title and happily agreed to let him use the gym. I had nothing to do with his training. He turned up with his own coach, Gordon Holmes, and just used the space, but this wound up Brendan even more.

Throughout the build-up to the fight, Brendan slated me and Herol in the newspapers. He even went on Sky Sports and called us both 'snakes', and said we were betraying Sheffield. I thought it was childish.

As the fight neared, Naz decided to pull a media stunt and turn up one day. I didn't really mind and found it funny. He arrived with full Ingle camp back-up, with Ryan Rhodes, Johnny Nelson and a few others tagging along. It was clearly just for publicity, so I let them get on with it. They were all wearing big, silly, false ears to take the piss out of Billy (he did have big ears) which struck me as especially comical as Naz had pretty big ears himself. Billy handled it all well. He was a good pro, a tough man and I had a lot of respect for him. Come fight night, Naz knocked Hardy out in round one. The kid was unbeatable back then.

I watched that fight in a bar in Spain, having taken a bunch of our kids over for a camping holiday. It was the first time I had done something like that and it was a fantastic experience for them. The majority of kids you get turning up to boxing gyms don't go on many holidays. It is a sport that always seems to attract youngsters from struggling families or challenging backgrounds, so it was something we thought would be good for gym spirit.

From my own junior days, I always fondly remembered the countryside walks we used to take with Brendan. Those were some of my happiest memories of him. It was an enjoyable trip, but hard work, as anyone who has ever looked after 20 junior boxers for a week can confirm.

When we got back to England, I was on such a high that I proposed to Hilary. We planned a wedding for Las Vegas that never happened. Then Hilary found out she was pregnant.

Suddenly it felt like Glyn Rhodes was growing up. I was approaching 40 years old, had a successful business and was settled in my home life. How the hell did all that happen? Our son Joseph was born on 6 January 1997. Almost a year later, our daughter Jorja arrived.

During this whole period, meanwhile, Herol had encountered problems getting his licence back. He passed all the necessary medicals and looked great in the gym, but there seemed to be a suspicion from the Board that after four years of retirement and his previous two fights both being defeats, he was not doing it for the right reasons. It took a lot of convincing but the BBBoC eventually gave him the green light.

Once Herol was licensed, he wanted a fight immediately. I was in two minds to some extent. He had always been such a fantastic talent but was this the right decision? To keep him happy, I set something up with a friend of mine called Pat Brogan, which resulted in a show at the Concord Centre in

Sheffield, with Herol topping the bill amid a blaze of local publicity.

Herol boxed an American called Terry Ford, who was really a blown-up light-middleweight, while Bomber was two pounds below the super-middleweight limit. Yet all through the fight, Herol never once had the kid in trouble. He won comfortably on points but there was no real devil in his work. Afterwards, I played the dutiful trainer and said all the things I was supposed to say to the media.

'Ring rust … needs rounds … class lasts forever … Herol will be better next time … timing was off … etc'.

When I got home and watched the video, though, I became very concerned. It was obvious there was something missing. I couldn't put my finger on what, a bit of speed, a bit of sharpness, a bit of timing, but he was just not quite there anymore. A few so-called experts had their say too in the press. They were quite scathing in their assessments of Herol's performance. It certainly wasn't the glorious comeback Bomber had hoped for.

I went round to Herol's house the following day because I felt we needed to have a heart-to-heart.

'Look, I'm sorry to say it, pal,' I said. 'But I honestly think it's best if you retire.'

He asked me to explain myself, so I said I just didn't think it was there anymore. I told him I didn't want to see a once-great fighter, who was also a close friend, humiliate himself by going on too long. Herol listened but, in truth, was not much moved. His heart was set on boxing on to the bitter end. I said I couldn't train him anymore but told him if he wanted to continue to use my gym, he would be welcome.

It was a difficult conversation to have, and I didn't feel great about it. You could see that some of my words hurt Herol, but it would have been easy for me to just continue training him and taking my ten per cent. My conscience wouldn't allow me to do that.

Herol asked around and arranged for London-based Dean Powell to train him, then scheduled a fight in London, against Craig Joseph from Bradford. Joseph was a game fighter, with a mixed record and a few decent wins, but was not really fit to lace Herol's boots.

We all went down to watch the fight and, as I took my seat at ringside, I got a message to say that Herol wanted to see me in the changing room. I went to find him, and he sheepishly asked if I would take him on the pads to warm up, which seemed a little strange. I told him I was happy to do so as long as it didn't step on Dean Powell's toes, but everyone seemed okay with it, so I took off my jacket and went through our usual routine. Once we had finished, I wished him luck and went back out to sit down.

As the fight started, a woman in the row in front of me turned to the man she was with, pointed at Herol and said,

'Look at this guy. He fights just like Naz!' I couldn't let that stand, so leaned over to explain to them that it was Naz who boxed like Herol. She accepted the information stoically.

As the action progressed, there were signs of the old magic, but Bomber got caught now and then. I found myself holding my breath every time he took a shot. Just like before, he won on points against an average kid, but to me he still didn't look like the real Herol Graham.

After I returned to Sheffield, I was approached by Dennis Hobson, who had built a reputation and a stable of fighters since he spoke to me all those years ago. He asked me to train a very promising young fighter he was managing called Clinton Woods. Woods was unbeaten in his first 14 fights and was very well-schooled, with a good amateur pedigree. He had taken some time away from the sport as a youth but turned pro in 1994 and was making a big local impression.

Clinton's arrangement with his previous trainer had ended, so he came to me to prepare him for his next fight, for the Central Area title against another Sheffield kid called Darren Littlewood. To make it extra spicy, Littlewood was trained and managed by Brendan. I must admit, this stirred something up inside me and provided extra motivation.

Clinton trained extremely hard and was a pleasure to work with. Unlike some of the other pros I coached, he had excellent fundamentals, and his feet and balance were always spot on. He had quick hands, too, and seemed to enjoy a scrap when it got nasty. I liked that.

The fight was set for a great little venue called the Pinegrove Country Club, where Dennis held regular events. A number of Clinton's fights had been there, and it was more or less his home venue.

There was some standard nonsense at the weigh-in, with all the Ingle crowd hanging around and trying to be intimidating. They always seemed to approach these things with a gang mentality, but Clinton was a quiet, humble guy and didn't let them get to him. He was also very tough, which helped.

On the night, in front of a raucous arena packed with Clinton's supporters, he dominated Littlewood and stopped him in the sixth. My only disappointment was that Brendan had not shown up. His son was in the corner instead. Not that I would have said too much to him, but it would have been nice afterwards to look him in the eye, just for a moment.

17

AGAINST MY advice, the Herol Graham comeback continued, with a fight I really felt was a step too far. Following his two unconvincing wins against journeyman types, Herol was boxing a pretty fearsome Canadian called Chris Johnson for the WBC international super-middleweight title at the Kensington Olympia in London.

Johnson was undefeated in 18 with plenty of knockouts, was a former Olympic bronze medallist and was widely expected to win comfortably, then go on to challenge for world honours. There had even been reports written in the media stating the fight should not have been sanctioned, that Herol was washed up and it was a dangerous mismatch.

I may not have been involved in Herol's training, but we had spent too long together for me to stay away, so I travelled down to London with a sense of trepidation. On the night of the fight, I tried to appear confident, because I didn't want Herol to see how concerned I was for him. I didn't give him much chance and just hoped he got through unscathed.

As soon as the bell rang, my heart leapt into my mouth. Herol got up on his toes and used the jab, while Johnson hunted him, waiting for openings, looking for the knockout. It was edge-of-the-seat stuff.

For some reason, after the first two rounds, I walked around to Johnson's corner to see if I could hear what his trainer was telling him to do. I thought maybe I might learn something I could pass on to Bomber. Within a few seconds of standing there I could tell that all was not well in the corner. They were frustrated by how hard Herol was to hit. So, I thought I'd help another way.

'Oi, Chris!' I shouted. 'You're not looking very good tonight, pal. What's wrong?' To my astonishment, Johnson stopped looking at his trainer, turned his head and stared straight at me. If there's one thing a chief second does not like, it's when your boxer stops listening to you, so I shouted something else. Johnson glared at me.

My antics seemed to be agitating all of them, so I stayed near the Johnson corner for the rest of the fight, shouting whatever I could think of between rounds to put him off. I may not have officially been part of Herol's camp, but if there was one way I could help him without trying too hard, it was by making a nuisance of myself.

I don't know how much impact I had but the longer the fight went on, the weaker Johnson became. Herol became more and more dominant as the rounds passed and in the end, Bomber applied intelligent pressure to win by eighth-round stoppage. He gave Johnson a real lesson from start to finish.

At that moment in time, this was an absolutely enormous upset which put Herol back in line for a world title fight at nearly 38 years old. Surely, he wasn't going to finally achieve his destiny, now? What an incredible story we were witnessing.

Back home in Sheffield, everyone was buzzing about Herol's performance. The media were a bit lukewarm and many of the experts who described the fight as a mismatch beforehand, now wisely stated that Johnson was a hype-job and clearly nowhere near as good as everyone thought. That annoyed me, as it was a way of avoiding giving Herol any credit. Bomber had rolled back the years and wiped the floor with a kid he was supposed to get steamrollered by. Why not simply appreciate that?

A lot of these boxing analysts have no clue what they're talking about and some of them, even some quite famous ones, have no background in boxing at all. I don't know what they think gives them the right to talk with such certainty about the sport. Anyway, the atmosphere in the gym was incredible and I had to hold my hands up and say publicly I had been wrong. Herol wasn't shot and was still capable of beating world-ranked fighters. I began working with him again in training, just little bits and pieces. Dean Powell was still his main man, but Herol had certainly done enough to show he deserved my time.

Bomber's rebirth generated a feeling that our gym was on the up and up, and that was confirmed by our involvement in a huge event, in December 1997 at Wembley Arena. Herol was set to defend his newly won WBC international super-middleweight title against American legend Vinny Pazienza. On the undercard, I had Clinton Woods fighting London-based traveller Mark Baker for the Commonwealth super-middleweight belt.

Pazienza, of course, arrived with an incredible backstory, having suffered a broken neck in a car crash and being told he would never walk again, then coming back to be world champion. He may have been past his best by that time, as so many of us had thought Herol was too, but we knew there was no way he was coming to England to lie down.

Once again, if I am honest, I was concerned for Herol. His performance against Johnson had been terrific, but could he repeat it, or had that been his last hurrah? The training went superbly, though, with a brilliant, collaborative spirit. Herol and Clinton were such different characters as Herol had always been flamboyant and unpredictable, while Clinton was quiet and self-effacing, but they combined well.

Herol spoke to me in the gym and asked if I would come back to work his corner for the Pazienza fight, but I told him it wouldn't be fair on Dean Powell. Regardless, I was still happy to help. So, on the night, the plan was for us all to be in the same changing room so I could be with both fighters, then I would go and work in Clinton's corner until the start of the last round, when I would run back to the changing room to get Herol ready.

The plan worked like clockwork, and I was so proud of Clinton that night. He put in a controlled and disciplined performance in a very tough bout. Baker kept coming after him and was strong and determined but Clinton built up a points lead with his superior jab and footwork. As agreed, at the start of the 12th, I wished Clinton well, then raced back to the changing room to get Herol ready, leaving Clinton and his team to finish the fight without me.

When I arrived back in the changing room, out of breath and sweaty, I found Herol sitting there alone.

'Fucking hell,' I said. 'That's the furthest I've run for years. Where's Dean?'

Herol shrugged. 'I dunno,' he said, so we started getting ready, just the two of us.

Through the walls we heard the announcer declare Clinton to be the new Commonwealth champion, which gave us both a little lift, but as I put Herol's gloves on, I could tell how tense he was. I rubbed his shoulders and reassured him that he would be okay.

Training had gone so well. All he had to do was go out and perform as he had in his last fight.

Glyn Rhodes the cheeky little chappie

A rare picture of Superman, my Grandad, who I idolised as a kid

Brendan Ingle, outside the St Thomas' gym. This is exactly how I remember him, from the days when I first started boxing.

Wrapping my hands in the changing rooms at St Thomas'

Brendan working my corner, during my amateur days.

Brendan with his original team of boxers, just before we all had to turn pro. I don't look very happy to be in the photo, for some reason

Herol was the star man at St Thomas' and the rest of us just had to accept that. Also in this pic are Brian Anderson, Walter Clayton and Winston Richards.

Power was one of my main attributes as a fighter. I was tall for a lightweight, and could bang a bit.

Have some of that! Me in one of my 65 pro fights.

Training in America with Angelo Dundee was a great experience. It was a privilege to do it so often.

With Brendan at my first wedding. Our relationship was still good in those days and I became Central Area champion two days later.

Sparring with future world champ Barry McGuigan, during a period when I still could have realised my potential as a fighter. If only, if only …

Knocking out Neil Foran, in a big upset, on a world title fight undercard. My moment of celebration was short lived as Foran didn't move for quite a while. It was such a relief when he sat up.

With Herol after one of my fights in London.

My great friend and business partner Dave Davies, with my two star fighters at the time, Richie Wenton and Herol Graham

Richie Wenton, on his way to beating Bradley Stone (RIP) in 1994. To collect my first British title as a trainer was fantastic, but events soon turned tragic. That's the yin-yang of boxing.

My first amateur show as a promoter, in 1995.

A pic with the man who created the 'Ingle' style, Bomber Graham, and the man who made it world famous, Naseem Hamed.

In the corner with Matt Mowatt during his fighting days. Matt has gone on to be a massive part of SBC ever since and one of my closest friends.

Bomber Graham against American legend Vinny Pazienza. Even right at the end of his career, Herol was capable of making fights like this look easy. Such a talented boxer.

I always enjoyed meeting boxing icons like the great Jake LaMotta. I could listen to their stories all day.

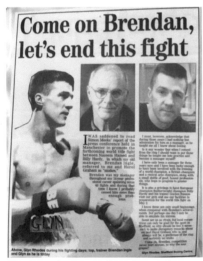

The letter I wrote to Brendan in the Sheffield Star. It was never my wish to be on bad terms with him, but he never responded, sadly.

In Florida with Harold Knight, Emanuel Steward's right-hand man, prior to Herol's last world title fight

How the other half live. Herol and myself are in the background, as we joined world heavyweight champ Lennox Lewis on his private boat before Herol boxed on his undercard in Atlantic City.

The first time I met Prince Charles, when he came to my gym on a state visit to Sheffield.

With Mexican legend Marco Antonio Barrera, who beat my fighter Richie Wenton in 1998. You have to respect someone of his ability.

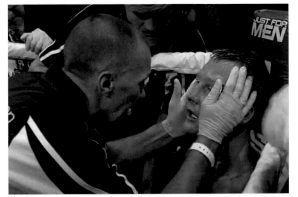

With Clinton Woods, before the last round of his last world title fight. He needed a KO to win, but I told him to keep his hands up and box. The most important thing is to get home safely.

With Angelo Dundee again. I saw him regularly until he died.

Being awarded an MBE for services to boxing will always be one of my proudest moments.

Collecting my MBE from Prince Charles

Visiting 'Deer Lake', Muhammad Ali's training base, on one of my many trips to America. I'm a keen student of boxing history as much as a fighter, trainer and manager.

As a trainer and manager, you spend so much time with your fighters, that you get attached. It's human nature. You can't help it.

Squaring up to world heavyweight champion, Anthony Joshua, when he used my gym. I found him to be very pleasant and respectful, a proper gentleman.

Scott Westgarth, full of life, with a smile on his face. This is how I like to remember him.

Walking to the ring with Scott Westgarth, fully focused on the task ahead.

With the doctor who was with me in the ambulance the night that Scott died. You naturally have a bond with someone after going through an experience like that.

Walking to the ring with Tommy Frank before a British title fight. Behind us are Matt Mowatt, John Fewkes and Sam Sheedy. SBC doing what it does best.

Even though Tommy won, I was overcome with emotion. The Scott Westgarth tragedy took a huge toll on me.

Walking around the Dam on the anniversary of Scott's death.

With Brendan, before he died. I'm so pleased we managed to make up before he passed away.

With Matt Mowatt again, 20 years after he retired from the ring and still by my side. You wouldn't want to run into those two in a dark alley …

A recent pic with Herol 'Bomber' Graham. The most gifted fighter I have ever seen and a lifelong friend. Even now, I still can't believe he never won a world title. It just wasn't meant to be.

With my wonderful kids, Jorja and Joseph.

With lightweight prospect Keanen Wainwright after a win in 2021. Also in the pic are Matt Mowatt (face covered) and Sam Sheedy. SBC is like a band of brothers.

Walking to the ring with my British flyweight champion Tommy Frank during coronavirus lockdown in 2021. Working with fantastic kids like Tommy gives me the motivation to keep going

We warmed up on the pads and he got nice and loose. Herol was always one of those fighters who clicked as soon as he started throwing his hands. It was all so natural to him and gave him a sort of peace. He even smiled. Like a lot of fighters, Herol was only truly happy when he was boxing. It took his mind off everything else.

Then, out of nowhere, the knock on the door arrived. It always jolts you, that knock. You're expecting it, but when it comes, it still manages to be a little startling. I was just as nervous as Herol, in truth, maybe more so, but walked to the ring with him. Dean Powell appeared as we reached the ring apron, so I took a back seat and let Dean run the corner.

As expected, it was a typical boxer versus puncher fight, the bull and the matador. Pazienza rushed in repeatedly and Herol stayed on the back foot and made him miss. This pattern suited Herol, as he didn't have to go looking for his opponent and won the first few rounds comfortably. Often, he made Pazienza look silly, but I knew Vinnie was a tough guy who would hang in there until he got an opportunity.

By the halfway point, Pazienza's mouth was cut, his nose was bleeding and he looked bruised around the eyes. Both boxers ended up in our corner in a clinch, so I shouted up to the American. 'Eh, Vinnie, you don't look so tough now, do you?'

In response, Pazienza leaned over the ropes and spat blood and snot all over me. Charming, although I guess I deserved it.

Incredibly, the fight continued in the same vein throughout and Herol took a wide points decision without any difficult moments. I kept waiting for him to get trapped in a corner or caught with a wild swing, but it never happened.

It was almost fairy-tale stuff, but that win meant Bomber was back in pole position to box for a world title, something nobody, including myself, had thought possible.

But success, when it comes, is not always simple. I was still relatively new to this side of the game and already had a top world contender and a Commonwealth champion to look after. Both Clinton and Herol were being pushed by their promoter, Dennis Hobson, who had tied some sort of deal in with Panos Eliadis, who handled the affairs of Lennox Lewis, the unified heavyweight world champion. That meant TV deals, more publicity, and more money for everybody but also required some tough decisions.

Herol was soon lined up to fight Charles 'The Hatchet' Brewer in Atlantic City, USA, for the IBF super-middleweight world championship, on the undercard of Lennox Lewis's WBC heavyweight defence against Shannon Briggs. The American broadcaster had made a deal with Sky in the UK, meaning the show at the Ice Arena in Hull, where Clinton was topping the bill, defending his Commonwealth title against David Starie, would be shown before the Atlantic City card, as part of the same pay-per-view package. This meant important, high-profile fights for my two top pros, taking place on the same night, 3,500 miles apart. Obviously, it was impossible for me to be at both.

I thought through my options, knowing that I would have to let somebody down, which wasn't nice at all. I did not manage or promote Clinton so would get ten per cent of his purse to go to Hull. On the other hand, I could go to Miami to train with Herol for the world title and get ten per cent of a larger purse. So that was one thing.

It had also already been decided that although the fight was in Atlantic City, Bomber would train at Miami Beach, one of my favourite places in the world. Other factors came into play, too. I had only trained Clinton for a few fights but had known Herol since we were both kids. In a way, Herol's story was intertwined with my own.

Clinton also had other people around him, guys who had worked with him from the past. There was a lot of jockeying for position going on and, in truth, I didn't like some of them. Not only that, but if I'm running a corner, it really annoys me when other people start talking. There should only be one voice, or the fighter gets confused and switches off. With Clinton's guys, it didn't always work like that.

The other consideration was that Clinton was young and in the early stages of his career. There was the opportunity for a long-term working relationship with the potential to go to the top of the game. That definitely held some appeal. On the other hand, age meant that even if Herol won, he was unlikely to have more than a couple of fights before retiring.

While I weighed up the pros and cons, Herol asked if I would go to New York with him for the press conference. I accepted and said I would make my choice when we got back.

So, I flew over with Bomber for the presser, which was held in Times Square. Although it was a big promotion, everyone was respectful, and Brewer didn't shoot his mouth off, which was nice.

During the press conference, an American journalist asked Herol if at 38 years and a few months old, he considered this his last chance for world honours. I didn't even listen to Herol's reply, because at that moment, the penny dropped. I knew that in my heart I had made my decision.

Clinton may have been a young man with a bright future ahead of him, but for my old pal Bomber, this was it. If he didn't make it count this time, he never would. He needed me more.

Sadly, there were some negative repercussions from this choice, as I thought there might be. Woods' team were bitterly angry with me and accused me of all sorts of things.

'What can I do?' I asked. 'Cut myself in half?' But they had no sympathy for my dilemma. So, I flew to Miami to work with Herol, and Clinton started working with Howard Rainey, another Sheffield trainer who came up from London.

Sadly, in my absence, Clinton struggled to make weight for his fight, eventually came in drained and depleted, and lost to Starie. I don't know the ins and outs of it, but apparently someone in Rainey's gym got him on creatine, a muscle-building supplement. As far as Woods' people were concerned, it was all my fault, of course.

Over in Miami, Herol and I shared a gym with Lennox Lewis, who was training with Emmanuel Steward, the famous head coach from the Kronk gym in Detroit.

It was a great camp for all of us, although Herol was a little moany and homesick, as he often was. Steward's right-hand man was a guy called Harold Knight, who I became very friendly with, and we all had some great fun with Lennox who thought our northern accents were hilarious.

The last day in Miami, Lennox hired a small boat and said he was taking us out for a meal before we all flew up to Atlantic City. We sailed up the waterway to a restaurant that was on the seafront and had a wonderful meal with Lennox Lewis and his mum, then got in the boat to sail back. I had to smile to myself. My last trip on a boat was when I had nicked one with my mates as a youngster. It seemed like I had come a pretty long way since then.

From there, it was everything you would expect from a big-fight experience. They sent a limousine to the airport to collect us. The hotel was like a palace and the area was thronging with media and fans waiting for the fight. 'This is it,' I thought. 'We've arrived.'

Over the next couple of days, I met and spoke with so many legends of the sport, from George Foreman and Marco Antonio Barrera, to Hank Kaplan and Tommy Hearns.

All I seemed to do at night was hang around the hotel reception. I couldn't sleep because the fight and the tactics we had formulated hung like a cloud over my mind. Every time I closed my eyes, my mind raced. As the big night neared, my wife flew out with Herol's girlfriend and my son, Joseph. I couldn't wait to see them and hoped it would relieve some of the tension.

Everyone's nerves were on edge, eased slightly after the weigh-in, which Bomber managed comfortably. We went for a walk and meal, and I couldn't help thinking how Herol's life would change forever if he won. The implications just seemed so huge.

18

THE NEXT morning, I woke early but laid there, staring at the ceiling until Herol woke up. I didn't want to wake him.

At breakfast everyone seemed a little happier. I think inside the anxiety of those situations, there's comfort in knowing the day has come. It's going to happen, what will be, will be, then you can all move on from it and continue with your lives. For a couple of months, we had been living in a bubble where everything was about Brewer v Graham. It gets on top of you after a while.

We didn't leave the hotel much that day. I walked the corridors a bit and went to the shopping centre that was part of the complex with Reagan Denton, a friend of Herol's (and a boxer) who had come over to support him. Herol stayed in the hotel room, sat on the edge of the bed, watching golf on TV.

We were out for several hours and when Reagan and I came back, Herol was still in exactly the same position.

'Fucking hell,' I said. 'Please tell me you've moved.'

Before we knew it, we got the call to say it was time to go, got our stuff together and walked to the convention centre, which was just down the Boardwalk from our hotel.

Once inside the venue, I remember thinking how big the place looked, and I thought of all the great fights that had taken place within those walls. Tyson vs Spinks, Cooney vs Spinks, Tyson vs Holmes, Gatti vs Ward and so many more. It was in places like this that boxing history was made.

The pre-fight rituals went well and by the time we were told when we would be on, Herol had been through a high-tempo pad session and was on fire, ready to go.

'Come on,' I said to him, softly. 'Let's do this.'

He nodded. 'It's my time.'

'It's your time, Bomber.'

The walk from the changing room to the ropes seemed to take an age and, once inside, the ring itself looked big. That suited us as space to move would play into Herol's hands. He did not seem so tense beforehand, as the MC made the introductions. There was a steadiness about him, like he was completely in the zone.

The fight began in typical Bomber Graham fashion. He jabbed and moved, while Brewer stalked. For the first few rounds, Herol was dazzling, putting on a perfect display of hitting and not being hit. Then in the third he caught Brewer off balance with a lovely shot and put him down. The champion climbed to his feet, only for Bomber to repeat the trick a minute or so later.

At this point, myself, and promoter Frank Maloney, who was helping out in the corner, were going nuts. It really looked like Herol would finish his man, but try as he might, he just couldn't quite get him out of there.

As the fight progressed, the big question was how long Herol's 38-year-old legs would continue to do all they needed to do. While many boxers retain punching power into their later years, speed, reflexes and stamina diminish with time and the fear was always that Herol would wilt in a high-pressure distance fight.

Sure enough, from about the sixth onwards, I could see him getting slower and slower. It was steady, excruciating, nail-biting drama, and I was praying he could hang on, but in round ten, Brewer buzzed Herol with a beautifully timed hook. I couldn't understand why Bomber didn't go down on one knee or hold on until his head cleared, but he just bobbed and weaved on the ropes. Brewer kept the shots coming, kept catching Herol, wouldn't let him off the hook, and the referee had no choice but to stop the fight.

As I jumped in the ring to console Herol, I felt devastated. Once again, he had been so close to winning a world title. Bomber always seemed to stumble at the last hurdle, even though less-talented fighters managed to go all the way. I suppose we had been wrong about his destiny all those years ago. Herol just wasn't meant to be a world champion.

Back in the dressing room, the atmosphere was sombre. Once we left to head back to the hotel, so many well-wishers approached us to congratulate Herol on a great fight. It was really tough to hear, but he smiled and thanked them and gave everyone his time, because that's what he was like, even when he was hurting. It was touching and sad and heroic all at once. What a guy and what a fighter, but that had to be the end of the road for him.

We skipped the after-party and all got up early the next morning to pack our things and leave for home. It was striking how once the fight was over, the VIP treatment stopped. On the way there we had been picked up by a limo but on the way home, we were all waiting at the bus station. I couldn't help but wonder if we would have been catching the bus had Herol won and become world champion.

After we got back from the States, things didn't look quite so exciting at the gym. I had lost Clinton Woods, who was even talking about retiring after his defeat. I didn't think he would, but I knew the bad blood that had been generated between me and his people meant he wouldn't come back to SBC. Herol was likely to retire. I hoped he would, for his sake, but that meant I had probably lost my two headline fighters.

There wasn't long to wallow in disappointment, though, as I was approached by a film producer who was planning to shoot a movie in Sheffield. He had been scouting for locations and asked if they could use my gym for a few scenes, and as a rehearsal space. They promised not to interfere with my boxing sessions, offered me £75 a day and I didn't have to do a thing. Easy money.

It wasn't all plain sailing and I fell out with the film people a couple of times, when I thought they were taking liberties, but overall, it was an interesting experience. In addition to the money, we were able to help ourselves to the on-location catering for free, which was a nice touch. Ultimately, the film went on to be a huge success, winning a host of awards. You may have heard of it. It was called *The Full Monty*.

After that, there was time for a mini-Herol Graham comeback, of sorts. A friend of mine called Jamie Reeves, who won the World's Strongest Man competition in 1989, had made a contact in Eastern Europe whose son was an amateur boxer. This guy wanted a professional opinion on his son and was willing to fund an all-expenses paid trip to Romania, for me and one guest, to make it work. I asked Herol if he was up for it, and we soon embarked on our next little adventure.

We flew out from East Midlands Airport in what can only be described as a tin can. It was the worst flight I had ever been on. I was wedged between Jamie and one of his equally enormous mates, the turbulence on the flight was terrible, and there were times I found myself praying, even though I'm not much of a believer.

We stayed in a shonky hotel and were introduced to the guy who had brought us over, who came across as a little unhinged to me. He drank vodka like it was water and kept giving us shots at every opportunity. I didn't want to offend him, so found pot plants or other places to pour it away in when he wasn't looking, which Herol found hilarious.

Eventually we were taken to the boxing club, which was quite a generous name for it as it didn't even have a ring. Loads of people from the local town had turned up to watch Herol do some training with the local boxer, and of course Herol loved it because they made a fuss of him. I took the boy, whose name was Totos, on the pads and found him typical of Eastern bloc fighters of the time. Strong, but robotic.

I then told Totos to spar a few rounds with Herol. As soon as the pair of them got their gloves on, the crowd started going mad, and Herol, being Herol, made it worse by winding a few of them up. The atmosphere was more like you would expect for a big fight rather than a spar and I began to get a bad feeling.

The boy's father ran into the other side of the building and came back with even more people. I decided I needed to manage expectations so stepped into the middle of the hall and tried to tell the crowd that it was only a sparring session. Of course, no one had a clue what I was saying, and they all just carried on cheering.

As soon as I called time, Totos ran at Herol and tried to knock him out. Herol did his thing, danced around and made the kid look silly. A couple of rounds passed of the kid swinging for the fences and missing, before I asked if anyone in the crowd would like to try and hit Herol, just like Brendan had used to do in the working men's clubs years before.

One guy, about 50 years old, who looked very tough, with a bashed-up face, stepped forward. It turned out he was the coach of the local amateur team. I whispered to Herol to take his time because the guy looked like he was taking this very seriously.

I shouted time and the fellow came out to spar, but shaped himself up like John L. Sullivan, as if he was boxing in 1895. Herol clocked on quickly that he would be able to toy with this guy, so put his hands behind his back, moved around and made him look an absolute mug. The more the chap tried to hit Herol, the more frustrated he got.

Herol was sticking his tongue out, dancing and humiliating the Romanian and the crowd rolled up laughing. I tried to save the local any more embarrassment by shouting time again, but as I walked over to him to take his gloves off, he nodded his head, aggressively, to say he wanted to carry on. All the while, Herol stood behind him, pulling faces, which the crowd also found hilarious.

As soon as the guy realised what Herol was doing, he completely lost his rag, and ran at Herol throwing punches from everywhere. At that point Herol decided he needed to teach him a proper lesson and hit the fella with a left uppercut to the body. All the colour drained from the bloke's face in a moment, and he dropped to his knees as if he just been run through with a sword.

Eventually, he got his breath back and climbed to his feet. Herol walked over to him and tried to shake hands, but the old bloke just pulled off the gloves and walked away. He clearly was not best pleased with what had gone on. As far as I was concerned, it was his fault. You can't spar a world-class fighter, try to take his head off and expect nothing to come back at you.

The crowd all wanted to shake hands with Herol and slap him on the back. We had no idea what they were saying, but everyone had clearly enjoyed Herol's exhibition. Then Jamie came over and said we should leave quickly. The boxing coach who Herol had humiliated had a local reputation as a bully and general nutcase and could very well return for some sort of revenge.

Herol just found it all funny. Bomber may not have been world champion, but he could definitely still put on a show.

19

BEFORE LEAVING Romania, we arranged for Totos to come to Sheffield, with the idea that he would use our gym for training and try to establish himself as a boxer. He came over soon after we returned, and we set him up in a little room next to the gym.

He lived there like a bear in a cave. The floor was always littered with drinks bottles and food packaging, but it suited him and was cheap.

Totos boxed for our amateur club for a while and did quite well, but things went awry when I received a phone call from South Yorkshire Police in the middle of the night. Apparently, they had picked him up prowling around the centre of Sheffield carrying a knife. As he had no family in England, I had to get up in the early hours and go to the police station, which I wasn't too pleased about. When I got there, I was shown the knife, which was more like a sword. The sort of thing hunters would use to strip the skin off a deer or something. The kid must have thought he was Crocodile Dundee.

By this time, the Burton Street site where I set my gym up had attracted a variety of other businesses and projects, turning it into a thriving, community hub. I like to think our success may have had something to do with that. There was even a young offenders' provision in the suite of rooms next to us, which seemed appropriate.

The transformation of the buildings, from disused primary school to symbol of Sheffield's regeneration, garnered a lot of media interest and we were informed, to our surprise, that we had been slated for a royal visit. Prince Charles would be coming to have a look, during his upcoming trip to Yorkshire.

As the royal visit came closer, regular checks were made, during which royal security officers came to do a dry run of where Prince Charles would be walking. They checked out the entire site and wanted to know where every door led to. As part of that, I had to give the names of everyone who would be in the gym on the day, along with registration numbers of all the cars that would be parked outside.

On the morning of the visit, they returned with sniffer dogs to check for hidden explosives.

They let the dogs run around the gym for a while, then I was told I wouldn't be allowed back in the gym until later, while they prepared everything. So, I went home for a shower and a bite to eat and planned to be back at 10am.

When I returned, I found the whole building in uproar. People ran around frantically, shouting into walkie-talkies. As I stepped through the door, I was grabbed by two security men.

'Is there anyone in the building whose name you haven't given to us?' one of them asked.

'No,' I replied. 'I can't think of anyone.'

'Come with us.'

I was strongarmed through my own gym, to the door of Totos' little bedroom.

'Who's this?' the security men demanded, pushing the door open.

Totos had just got out of bed and was sat there in his underwear. There were a couple of discarded pizza boxes on the floor next to him. I had forgotten all about him.

As a result, I was bundled off and interrogated pretty vigorously for about 20 minutes. There was a lot of suspicion about who Totos was and what he was doing there. The idea that I had a young Romanian boxer living in a cupboard in the gym didn't seem to be one they found especially believable.

'Who is he?' they kept demanding. 'How did he get on site?'

'Guys, I'm so sorry, but as I've already told you, he didn't get on to the site. He lives here.'

The whole situation wasn't helped by the fact that Totos couldn't speak English, so when they tried to question him, he just shrugged, grinned and looked shifty.

For a while, I thought Prince Charles' visit might be scrapped, but after a lot of brisk talking and hard stares, they gave me the benefit of the doubt, in that Totos probably wasn't a terrorist or assassin, and decided to proceed, as long as he left the site. I watched through a window as he sloped away across the playground, through the cordon of security men out there, all eyeing him up and down. I couldn't help but laugh. The whole thing seemed so ridiculous.

The closer we got to the allotted time for the prince's arrival, the more the tension built. I could understand that. It was these guys' job to keep the prince safe and if anything happened on their watch, there would be hell to pay. When he finally walked into the room, it felt like such a surreal moment. He appeared in the doorway, smiling, looking a lot smaller than he did on TV or in newspapers and everyone just stood still, in silence, waiting to be approached.

When he got to me, he shook my hand very firmly.

'It's a tough sport, boxing, isn't it?' he asked.

'It most certainly is,' I replied.

He went on to speak to me for quite a while, saying that he used to play rugby when he was younger, which was also tough, although he hadn't enjoyed it. He said his great-grandfather had been a big boxing fan.

Afterwards, I must admit I was buzzing. All the lads from the gym asked what it had been like to meet him, and I had to say the whole experience did feel like a privilege. How many people get to shake hands and have a chat with the future King of England?

A few days after the prince's visit, I rang my old pal Dave Davies, the guy who had done so much to help me get my training career up and running, to tell him about the whole thing. At the end of the conversation, Dave said he had to go into hospital for some check-ups, which I didn't concern myself with too much. Then, a few days later, Hilary had an accident in the garden, so I took her down to A&E. While we were waiting to see the doctor, I took the opportunity to pop up and see Dave.

When I got to his room, his wife Linda was there.

'Hi, Glyn,' she said. 'Great to see you. He doesn't have long left, I'm afraid.'

I couldn't believe it. Dave had been such a great friend to me and so instrumental in my work. Apparently, he had had kidney problems for years and by this point, there was nothing anyone could do.

After his funeral, I had a boxing show at the Grosvenor Hotel in Sheffield to organise, which is exactly the sort of thing Dave would have got involved with. I went about my business with a heavy heart for that one.

The show was a dinner event and went well, although it turned sour afterwards, when the three businessmen who came on board with me as co-promoters got sniffy over money. It's incredible how often people seem nice, but as soon as there's money on the table, they show their true colours. I guess this happens in all walks of life but seems very prevalent in the fight game.

There's a certain kind of man who's very attracted to the world of boxing, the kind of bloke who looks up to tough guys and likes to hang around with them, although he could never really be one himself. The sort of people who get a little thrill from the language and mannerisms of violence, but not violence itself. If you work in the business side of boxing, a lot of the characters who end up coming on board as investors are like this and the trouble is that although they are drawn to the sport, they don't understand it.

That experience, along with a few others, led me to apply for a seat on the Central Area Council of the British Boxing Board of Control. The deeper my involvement in the game became, and by then I was in pretty deep, it made sense to get an influence on as many aspects of the business as possible. My application was successful and before my first meeting, I was told by the secretary, Harry Warner, to keep my mouth shut until I knew what was going on. That was sound advice, as soon, I would find myself confronting Brendan across that table.

20

WITH MY status within the boxing scene developing, and my seat on the area council making me feel like part of the establishment, I got a phone call telling me that none other than Richie Wenton wanted to come back to the gym again.

Since losing to Belcastro on that awful Italy trip, Richie had gone back to Brendan's, again. I wasn't a huge fan of the way he kept bouncing between gyms, but something about Richie always made it hard to say no to him.

The day after that phone call, Richie turned up at my house. I rolled my eyes, but of course, I let him in, and he told me some major news. He had been awarded a world title shot against the Mexican legend Marco Antonio Barrera and needed someone to prepare him. The fight was slated to take place on the undercard of Naseem Hamed's world championship defence against Wayne McCullough in Atlantic City and the gist I got from Richie was that he wasn't happy playing second fiddle to Naz.

Over at St Thomas,' Brendan's main focus was on Hamed, who by this time was well on the way to becoming a global superstar. You couldn't really blame Brendan for that, but Richie thought that by coming back to SBC he would be top dog and get more focused, individualised training.

All the times I had promised myself I would never work with him again went through my mind in a handclap, but I took him back. Suddenly, I had another huge night of world championship boxing in Atlantic City to prepare for.

I knew from the beginning that this one would have extra spice. Brendan would be there, with Hamed and his people. We would be sharing facilities with them. The ongoing story of our master and pupil feud was about to get yet another new episode.

Richie hadn't changed and I can't say I was surprised when the training camp wasn't easy. It was so hard to get him to knuckle down and do the stuff he needed to do, even when preparing for a massive fight. It became a battle in the gym every day with myself and Herol trying to keep Richie on track. By the time we flew to the States, I was worn out mentally.

'Never again,' I promised myself as we boarded the plane. I'm not even sure I believed it anymore, but it still reassured me to think it.

Just as before when I visited the same city for Herol's fight, we stayed in a fabulous hotel. Naz's people had organised a gym inside the hotel, so we didn't need to travel to train. After arrival, I saw Naz and Brendan most days. Brendan would just pretend I wasn't there and blank me, while Naz usually just nodded. I knew most of Naz's entourage, but it was difficult for any of them to be seen talking to Herol and I. We were regarded as the enemy.

The first day there, before lunch, Herol and I were using the steam room in the hotel spa, when from behind the closed door we heard Brendan's voice, so knew he was coming in, too. I added some more water to the coals and by the time Brendan opened the door, the steam was so thick he couldn't see us. Slowly he padded his way over to the bench where Herol was sitting and lowered himself down.

Once the steam thinned a little, Brendan looked sideways, realised he was sitting next to Bomber, said, 'Oh, for Christ's sake,' then stood straight up and walked out. Both of us fell about laughing like schoolboys.

For both Herol and I, we dealt with the awkwardness light-heartedly, although for both of us there was also sadness. I honestly didn't think there was any need for Brendan to carry on like that. I was more than happy to say hello and be polite and I know Herol felt the same.

Very quickly, the laughter stopped, and the bad blood turned sour, though. The first time we went down to the gym in the hotel, I asked the guy at the door what time Richie would be able to train. He looked up at me, in that very polite, American, service industry way, all bright eyes and white teeth, and said,

'I'm sorry sir, but this is a private facility solely for the use of Prince Naseem Hamed.'

I tried to explain who we were, but he was very insistent. I asked him to check with Naz the next time he was in, to clarify the situation. I was certain he had got his wires crossed.

The next day, we returned. Same guy, same smile, 'I'm sorry sir. I spoke to Mr Hamed personally and he confirmed that this gym is for his use only.'

'What a fucking shithouse,' I said. The guy raised his eyebrows. 'Sorry pal,' I went on. 'Not you.'

Hasty arrangements were made for us to use a New Jersey police gym downtown instead. We were picked up from the hotel every day in a minibus and driven there along with Danny Romero, a former world champion, who was challenging the South African champion Vuyani Bungu for the IBF world super-bantamweight title on the same show.

This all left a bad taste in my mouth towards Naz. I hadn't really had a problem with him before. I couldn't see any grown-up reason why he would disallow us from using the same gym. We were happy to work around him and use it when he wasn't there, after all. The differences were between me and Brendan, not his fighters. It all just seemed incredibly petty and spiteful, especially as Richie was being punished, along with me, and Richie had trained with Brendan and Naz, too.

The good thing about training at the police gym was that Barrera was also using it and I managed to watch him a few times. His team didn't know who I was until the press conference the night before the fight, so I got away with it. I was very impressed with him and knew then that Richie was up against it. Barrera was a supreme pressure fighter and capable of going up through the gears in a flash. We would need a very careful game plan. This somehow developed into a big disagreement in our camp.

Having watched Barrera up close, my plan for the fight was for Richie to jab and move for the first few rounds, try to frustrate the champ, then see how the fight developed after that. Richie, God bless him, wanted to go out and have a tear-up from round one.

I couldn't see any possibility of Richie winning like that. If you watched Barrera's previous fights, the only guy who had beaten him was Junior Jones, who had used boxing and movement. Richie was a good technical boxer, with decent speed. Why not try to use those attributes? Getting in close and trading would play right into the Mexican's hands, as far as I was concerned.

Richie started ranting on about how he was going toe to toe with Barrera and was going to shock him. Me and Herol just started laughing. Our laughter seemed to gee him up more and I suddenly thought, 'I don't need this.' Richie wasn't listening to sense.

All the Richie Wenton nonsense I had put up with over the years came flooding back. All the times I had vowed never to work with him again. Now here we were for the biggest fight of his career, and he's paying no attention to what I'm telling him.

I turned to Herol and said, 'I'm off. I don't need to listen to this shit.'

So, I left the gym, made my own way back to the hotel and stewed in my own juices. Later that night, both Bomber and Richie came to my room. Richie apologised and said he would try to fight my way. I don't think he meant it. He just said it because he wanted me to stay.

When the fight came around, there was an eerie familiarity about the whole thing. The weigh-in was held in the same space and we had the same changing room as we'd had for Herol's tilt at Brewer. An hour or so before we were due to ring-walk, I wrapped Richie's hands, then went to the other changing room for the standard ritual of watching the opponent getting his hands wrapped.

It was a strange feeling. I was there in a professional capacity but also found myself a little excited to be in the changing room of Marco Antonio Barrera, who was already considered a great of the sport. He had his corner team and a small entourage in there, all steely-eyed Mexicans straight out of a Sergio Leone Western.

I noticed the tape they were using was some sort of plastic stuff, so plucked up my courage to speak up.

'I don't like this tape,' I said.

Barrera's trainer looked at me, coldly. 'This is the same tape we always use in Mexico,' he replied.

'Well, we're not in Mexico, are we pal?' In for a penny, in for a pound.

He had almost finished both of Barrera's hands, but I told him to stop, and he started mumbling to the other guys in the room. I explained to the official that the tape was wrong. The official inspected it and agreed with me.

Suddenly everyone started shouting in Spanish and waving their hands around, while I just stood there feeling pleased with myself. If nothing else, I had managed to disrupt their preparations a bit. Eventually Barrera's trainer said he didn't have any more bandages or tape, so they had to leave the wrappings on.

'Guys, its fine,' I said. 'I've got plenty. I'll lend you some.'

The whole area went quiet, and all the Mexicans stared me down, but I stuck to my guns and made them cut the bandages off Barrera's hands and start the whole process again.

As we walked out later, we were told that they had lost Richie's music. In his heightened state, Richie flew right off the handle and started walking back to the dressing room. There were a few minutes during which I was afraid he would pull out, but I managed to convince him to turn back, and we walked to the ring with some random song playing that he hadn't chosen. To me, it didn't matter, but Richie really seemed to let it upset him.

I was worried, as I always am before any of my boxers' fights but especially so, as it looked to me like the occasion was getting to Richie. When Barrera stared at him during the ref's instructions, I felt that Richie had frozen.

From the first bell, Barrera came out throwing bombs with both hands. True to form, Richie didn't move around and stay out of the way. He stayed in range and fired back. When he came back after round one, he was already bruised and marked up.

It was more of the same in the second. Richie tried to throw a few more punches but didn't have the power to get Barrera's respect.

By the end of that one, I actually thought about pulling Richie out. He was banged up pretty badly already. The only reason I didn't was that it felt a bit insulting to Richie to retire him after just two rounds of his first world title challenge.

So, I let him go out for round three, but Richie was never going to win a war against Barrera. He got through with a few of his own punches but wilted under pressure. Eventually, he went down twice from body shots, then got stopped at the end of the round.

I did my best to make sure he was okay in the changing room. He just sat with his head down, staring at the floor. The atmosphere was like a morgue, as it always is after a heavy defeat. It was always going to be a big task to beat Barrera, but Richie's stubbornness hadn't helped.

Once I was sure that the only damage Richie suffered was to his pride, I went out with Herol to watch Naz fight Wayne McCullough. McCullough was tough and Naz beat him on points, only to be abused by the crowd, who spat and threw things at his mother. They were ugly scenes, but I found myself reflecting on the two fights I had watched. It looked to me like Naz had lost a bit of his sparkle. If he ever fought Barrera, I reckoned he would struggle.

21

EVEN AFTER all that, my experiences with Richie Wenton were not quite finished. Six months after the Barrera fight, I worked with him one last time, for his comeback against the wily journeyman, Peter Buckley. After picking up that win, Richie left the gym again, as he had done before.

Strangely, I sensed, as he walked away after the Buckley fight, that we were done. I had promised myself so many times to finish our professional relationship, but never had. At that point I could just tell it had reached its natural end. Over the following couple of years, Richie moved up to featherweight, lost a British title challenge to Gary Thornhill, then took on the formidable Scott Harrison for the Commonwealth title and was stopped in four, in what proved to be the last act of his career.

On reflection, I knew I had had some great moments with Richie. For a kid who changed trainers nearly as regularly as he changed his pants, I also took satisfaction from all the time we had together and the fact he kept coming back to me. Richie was a kid with a restless heart, but nonetheless we had been good for each other.

With Richie gone, I was able to focus on some of the newer lads at my gym. It was a time in which I had no major stars like Richie, Clinton or Herol, but lots of solid pros. One in particular, a middleweight called Matt Mowatt, was great to manage. He was never going to be a world champion but had enough spirit to be one ten times over.

He had been locked up in Strangeways prison when the infamous riot broke out and was one of the prisoners sat on the roof, throwing slates at the police below, as shown on TV news. He had been in the British army but got kicked out for fighting. He had chinned his mother's boyfriend because he hit her, then ran away from the police to France, where he joined the Foreign Legion. Somehow, he managed to get thrown out of that, as well, then in the manner of lost souls everywhere, found his way to boxing. Matt and I formed a great bond, very quickly, which would last throughout his short career, and beyond. When he retired from the ring in 2001, he came to work with me at the gym and has been there ever since.

Towards the end of 1998, I got a phone call from Nabeel Hamed, Naz's brother, which intrigued me. He asked about the chance of Naz training at SBC. I asked why he would want to and was told he had sacked Brendan.

'Oh, blimey,' I thought. 'Here we go.'

It was explained that Naz and Brendan had fallen out, because of things that had been written in a book which Brendan was having published. I had also heard on the grapevine, as had many other people, that Naz and Brendan were drifting apart due to money issues. Naz had been earning multi-million purses for a while, so there was plenty at stake.

I had the feeling Nabeel expected me to be flattered, but the truth was I would have had more respect for Naz if he had picked the phone up himself. I had known him since he was a young kid, after all.

So, Nabeel launched into this sales pitch, telling me how all Naz's family respected me, and they didn't agree with the things Brendan said about me. All the stuff that happened with the gym in the Atlantic City hotel was all Brendan's fault and they didn't like it and blah, blah, blah.

I didn't really believe him, and I don't think he thought I believed him, but at the same time, I knew Naz needed to find a gym, quickly. He was due to fight Paul Ingle in Manchester and my place was the only one around where Naz would feel comfortable.

I still respected Naz as a fighter and he was the biggest name in British boxing at the time, so I agreed that he could use the gym, provided he paid like everyone else. I also knew, of course, that this arrangement would make Brendan hate me even more than he did already. By that point, I had got used to this. No matter what I did, it seemed Brendan had a problem with it.

Naz's brothers had some t-shirts printed with 'Prince Promotions proudly sponsor Sheffield Boxing Centre' on them and they gave me two grand, which was nice. I was asked to wear the t-shirts whenever I was working corners for my other fighters. They also bunged me Adidas trainers and tracksuits they received through Naz's sponsorships.

Things began well, but a couple of weeks after Naz started training in my gym, I got a phone call from Riath, the eldest of the three brothers, asking if I could come up to their office.

When I arrived, I found Riath behind a desk, Naz sat on the sofa and Nabeel standing by the wall. It all felt weirdly formal.

I was asked to sit down. Naz looked at me, deadly serious and said, 'Glyn, we've got a problem.'

'What's up?' I asked.

'I need the gym from 4 to 5pm all to myself,' he said.

'What do you want me to tell all the kids that come to train straight after school?'

He just looked at me.

'Do you want me to say they can't train because Naz wants the gym to himself? That would look terrible for you. To be honest, I'm not prepared to do it, anyway.'

'Look, Glyn,' he said. I assumed he was about to tell me the big, convincing reason why this needed to happen. 'I was on the bag the other day and there was a kid on the next bag.'

'Right,' I said, wondering where this was heading.

'And the thing is, Glyn.' Naz narrowed his eyes. 'He was wearing jeans.'

There was a brief pause while I waited for him to continue, but it seemed he had finished.

'Okay?'

'I'm world champion, Glyn.'

'And?'

'It don't look good when I'm training and there's someone at the side of me boxing in fucking jeans.'

What made the whole exchange even weirder was that I knew who he was talking about. The kid was a good kid, who had forgotten his shorts that day. He had even asked me if I had any spares, but I didn't, so he trained in his jeans.

It seemed to me that Naz had forgotten where he came from. I had known him since he started with Brendan at seven years old, and he certainly didn't always have designer boxing gear to train in. He was from a working-class family in Wincobank. Who did he think he was?

I wasn't prepared to cave in over something so ridiculous, so the Hameds came up with their own solution, by renting a vacant room at the side of my gym, in the old school. They got Mike Goodall, who used to do a lot of emceeing at boxing shows, to come up and erect them a full-size ring. From then on, Naz trained in his own little gym next door to mine.

Once they were inside, they would lock the door so that none of my kids could go in. It was all quite sad, really.

I actually found myself making excuses for him, saying it was his new trainer or the promoter who didn't want people watching, but as a result of this whole episode, Naz stopped being so popular with the youngsters at my place.

During this whole period, there were constant stories in the papers about Brendan and Naz, and often Brendan's relationship with his other fighters too. Then further articles about the relationships between all of them, individually. The Ingle gym had become the centre of a great deal of Sheffield's sporting coverage, as at the time it was producing so many top fighters.

One of these articles, which was much discussed, was about some money Naz claimed was owed to him by Johnny Nelson. Naz said it was a loan. Johnny said it had been given as a gift and it seemed they were arguing between themselves about it. We had spoken about the story in our gym, in the same way people all over Sheffield had.

I took some kids down to Devon on one of our boxing excursions and while I was down there, I was told by Lee Gostollo, who looked after things at SBC while I was away, that Johnny Nelson had phoned the gym angrily.

Apparently, Johnny said that I was telling people Naz owes him money and he made some sort of unspecific threat. 'You tell Glyn, that when I see him, the shit's gonna hit the fan!' Or something like that. By this time Johnny had rebuilt his career and was European cruiserweight champion, so Lee took the implications of that very seriously.

Once again, I found all this pretty silly. The dispute was between Naz and Johnny and the whole thing had been in the papers. If I had said anything, it was only to comment on what I had read. It angered me that Johnny would phone the gym while I was away and speak to someone else instead of me about a matter like that. Who he really needed to speak to, of course, was Naz.

Immediately, I phoned Herol Graham and told him I wanted Nelson's number. Bomber gave me his number and I called straight away. I was shaking with rage as I rang him but tried to stay calm. From the way he answered the phone, I could tell I was the last person he expected to call him.

We exchanged a few words and he said, 'When I see you face to face, we will sort it out.'

'I will be home tomorrow,' I replied. 'I'll call you and we can do it then.'

I laid in bed that night thinking about how to handle this Nelson nonsense. The guy was twice my size and a few years younger than me, but he was never someone I would have tipped to pass a gut check. I had known him since he was a little kid and did not believe he had the nerve to take me on, if it came to it.

All the way home I thought how lame it was for a champion boxer to act tough on the phone. I wanted to see how tough he would be in person.

I arrived home, walked in the house and immediately called Nelson several times without answer. I left messages on his answering machine, but I never heard a thing back. God loves a trier, so I got his mobile number off Herol too and rang that repeatedly, but no answer again. Throughout the rest of the day, I must have phoned him 20 times, and left multiple messages, but he never once had the courage to pick up or return my call.

I gave up in the end, knowing that our paths would cross one day. The boxing scene is quite a small world, and you tend to bump into the same faces again and again. Part of me felt that this was all an outgrowth of my fall-out with Brendan. Fighters like Johnny had grown up with this feud going on and internalised it. As far as they were concerned, Glyn Rhodes was there to be shot at, but Johnny Nelson had no right to threaten me.

Our time would come. I knew it.

22

AT THE time, I had a super-welterweight boxing with me called Reagan Denton, who had just completed all his pro forms and was about to make his debut. Fate intervened and Reagan's fight, against another novice called Pedro Thompson from Birmingham, was scheduled to take place on the undercard of Johnny Nelson's world title fight against Bruce Scott in Sheffield on 15 May 1999. Nelson had won the WBO cruiserweight world title by then and the bout with Scott was due to be his first defence.

I knew this event would be like walking into the lion's den. All the Ingle team would be there to support Nelson, but there would be a fair crowd from my gym too. If things went the wrong way, there was a chance it could all get out of hand.

I arranged to meet everyone at the Stakis hotel in Sheffield, where the weigh-ins were being held. As I walked up to the entrance of the hotel with Reagan, a car pulled up beside us, so I looked inside to see none other than Johnny Nelson driving with local boxer Dave Coldwell in the passenger seat. Coldwell was as cocky as Nelson, even though he's a tiny little fella. I walked up to the car and spoke to Johnny.

'Do you want to sort this out before we go inside?' I asked him. I can't say I was shocked when he replied, 'Go away. You're not worth it,' then drove away to park his car. That was actually the time to do something like men. We could have settled things, just the two of us, but Johnny didn't want to know.

I walked into the hotel with Reagan and sat with him in the foyer. Before long, Nelson and Coldwell strutted in through the door, surrounded by arse-kissers. Nelson stuck his chest out and stared at me. It was all very theatrical and clearly for the benefit of his hangers-on, especially as he had just had the chance to confront me in the car park and turned it down.

I wasn't in the mood for a childish staring contest, so I stood up and walked over to him. His friends all gathered around, but again nothing happened. He pointed at me melodramatically and said, 'I'll deal with you after the fight.'

'Why didn't you deal with me outside a few minutes earlier?' I asked.

He said nothing.

Nelson's wife then stepped forward to defend her husband's honour, by shouting something or other, but I was too focused on Johnny to really register what she said. By this point, we were standing very close together, so I felt it was only a matter of time before something went off. I didn't want to throw the first punch, especially with him having a title defence the next day, but I also kept myself ready. He may have been well known as a bottler, but he was 6ft 2in and broad across the shoulders. If he had found some courage from somewhere and hit me on the chin, he would probably have knocked me out. After the way he behaved, that would have been so embarrassing for me.

And then, it all happened at once. He leaned a little closer, so I made the first move and tried to grab him, but he panicked as I went for him. There was a lot of pushing and shoving but nothing much really happened, other than Nelson's wife managing to blindside me and smack me in the mouth. At least someone in the Nelson family had some balls.

We got pulled apart and there were people between us. He was about 10ft away from me, bouncing around on his toes, shadow boxing. It was embarrassing to see.

He started shouting what he was going to do to me before people led him away. As he was taken up the stairs, he was screaming 'Hold me back, hold me back!' At the same time, you could tell he was walking off quite happily. It was all fairly pathetic and done to try to save face while avoiding any sort of real confrontation.

That was the end of things for a short while. An official said I couldn't go upstairs, and I replied that they should weigh my kid in first, then I would leave and there would be no more trouble.

So, I sat in the hotel bar, trying to stay out of the way, while Reagan and his mates went to the weigh-in, which was in an adjoining room. Before long, the door to the weigh-in room opened and Johnny Nelson walked out, with Ryan Rhodes and a few other kids in tow. They zeroed in on me straight away, so I stood up trying to look confident. Ryan stepped forward.

'I've heard you've been talking about me, too,' he said, pointing his finger. I was backed into a corner by about five of them and could see it was going to be a fight just to get out. We were making quite a scene. This was it. The big moment. Me against the Ingle boys. They were all there, posturing and snarling, but still not actually doing anything.

'Come on, then!' I said. 'You're never going to get a better chance to give me a bashing while I'm on my own, are you?'

They all just stood there. By this stage, Brendan had found his way into the bar and was shouting that I should be thrown out and banned from the next day's show and anything else he could think of.

So, in the middle of this whole, absurd kerfuffle, one of the hotel staff approached me and said it would be best if my made my way out of the hotel. The Ingle crowd parted for me to go, so I left. And that was that.

The whole thing, from start to finish, was nothing. Handbags at ten paces.

News of this weigh-in bust-up spread around town very quickly, but in truth, nothing much happened. It was mostly shouting, with a bit of jostling. I'd had scarier encounters on the school playground.

I did attend the following evening as well and stayed around to watch some of Johnny's fight, which was top of the bill, just to make a point. As usual, it was like watching grass grow, so I waited for the end of a round, then picked up my bag and walked very deliberately through the crowd and out of the venue. Maybe that was me being a little childish, but I wanted everyone to know that I was there and not intimidated by the Ingle boys and their gang tactics.

After a short while, I received a letter from the BBBoC, stating they received a complaint from Brendan Ingle, and summoning me to London for a hearing. It was claimed that I had assaulted Nelson at the weigh-in. 'Assaulted' was a colourful description for what had effectively been a bear-hug, but Brendan always did have a gift for storytelling.

The letter also stated I could have a solicitor to represent me and should bring along any relevant witnesses, as Mr Ingle and Mr Nelson would be doing the same. You would have thought I was on a murder charge.

The week before the case was to be heard, I was in Naz's office. Riath spoke to John Morris, who was the general secretary of the BBBoC at the time and Morris said he didn't think it would be anything more than a wrist slap. Naz overheard the conversation and offered to send his barrister with me, which I appreciated, especially as the whole reason all this had happened was because of Naz.

When I arrived in London for the hearing, I was surprised to find it being led by Leonard 'Nipper' Read, a former high-ranking police officer who had famously locked up the Kray twins back in the sixties.

Various statements were made, and I gave a short explanation of my time with Brendan and what had happened since. Johnny then spoke up and said he thought all the bad feeling was because I was jealous of him. That when we were both growing up in Brendan's gym, I used to bully him, but now he was a world champion and I resented it.

As was so often the case with this lot, I couldn't believe what I was hearing. Yes, he was world champion but was also a guy who was going down in history for two of the most cowardly world title challenges ever (against Carlos De Leon in 1990 and James Warring in 1992) and who couldn't fill a phone box if he fought in his own back yard. I sat there, remembering how everyone in the gym knew him as a kid who lacked heart.

After Johnny, my witnesses were given short shrift, before Brendan was allowed to speak. As expected, Brendan's evidence turned into an epic fable that seemed to go on for hours. At last, when it was all over, Read and the other officials went away to deliberate, then returned to say they had considered the matter very carefully and decided to fine me for bringing the sport into disrepute. Johnny received no sanction whatsoever.

I travelled back to Sheffield fuming. The whole thing had felt like a kangaroo court and a blatant case of bias. Over the next few weeks, I had all sorts of things going through my mind, as to how I might get my own justice.

23

THIS SEEMED to be a time in my boxing life when events in the ring were constantly being superseded by events out of it. Not long after the Johnny Nelson fiasco, Paul 'Silky' Jones was entering the last stages of his career having been stopped by the fearsome Londoner Jason Matthews, for the Commonwealth title.

Paul came back to the gym, introduced me to a bloke called Bernard from Rotherham, who was some sort of new business associate of his, and asked if I would be interested in promoting his comeback fight.

'Don't worry about the money,' Paul said. 'Bernard has plenty of money.'

Paul kept referring to Bernard as his sponsor, but at one point Bernard took me to one side and asked to be called Paul's 'business manager'. I could tell straight away that he was another of these boxing hangers-on. More than anything, he wanted to be liked by fighters, to be 'in' with them. It was hard to have much respect for him.

I told Paul it might be hard to get an opponent for him as he was a former world champion, but I agreed to give it a go. Heavy going as it was, we organised everything between us and set up a show in Rotherham, at Herringthorpe Leisure Centre. Paul's first comeback fight would top the bill. He was set to box a tough kid called Ganny Dovidovas, while some of my other fighters would fill out the undercard: Paul Owen, Kevin England, Gary Wilson and Jason Barker.

The show was successful, but Bernard overspent massively on the promotion, paying for all sorts of razzmatazz, like disco lights and dancing girls. God knows why. The venue only held 800 people, meaning takings were limited. Despite his financial losses, that one only whetted his appetite and he asked me to help him promote another Silky Jones show as soon as possible.

We set a date for July. Again, it was set to be mostly my fighters on the bill, while Paul seemed to be enjoying the vibe of working with Bernard. He turned up in the gym with a new trainer, who had no clue what he was doing at all. Apparently, Bernard had sorted things out for him.

A rift began to grow in the gym, as Paul was working separately with this new guy, with Bernard tagging along like a puppy. No one wanted to spar with Paul as he was going so hard, so Bernard had to bring in private sparring. Even with that, I didn't like what I was seeing. Paul was super aggressive in sparring but the guy he was paying needed the money too much, so put up with it. Stuff like that can be dangerous. A lot of people in the gym weren't happy with what was going on and I had lots of people coming to see me and complaining.

It was a difficult time in lots of ways and got to the point that I was going to have it out with Paul and explain that I wasn't happy, before fate intervened. I was on my way into the gym, planning what I was going to say to Paul, stopped off at the bank and got hit by a car, which laid me up for a few weeks. At least that got me out of the poisonous atmosphere at SBC, although I knew it was all still going on.

A week or so before the show I had recovered well enough to go back to work and received a phone call saying that Paul Jones' opponent had pulled out with an injury. Bernard almost had a heart attack, so I sat him down and explained that these things happen in boxing, and you have to roll with it. We would just have to pay to get another opponent.

I rang around frantically, but things were not looking good. I began to have conversations about the possibility of cancelling the show. All the lads on the card were upset until Jason Barker piped up. 'Don't cancel the show, I'll fight him.' he said.

At first, we all laughed, but Jason was serious. After I thought about it for a while, I came to the conclusion that it wasn't such a bad idea after all. Jason was the right weight, had a mixed record as he fought away from home a lot, but could really fight when he wanted to.

So, I rang Bernard and told him our options were to cancel the show or put Jason Barker in with Paul. Neither Bernard nor Paul were happy with the new opponent but there was nothing anyone could do. It was Jason or nothing.

So, the fight was on. Paul stopped training at my gym as he didn't want to be around Jason in the build-up. Frankly, that was a relief for everyone. Jason started talking it up from his side too and it generated some good local publicity. Everyone seems to love a grudge match.

Local TV came down to the gym to interview Jason, which he loved. He got hold of a poster of Paul and tore up it in front of the camera. The TV people asked whose corner I would be in, and I replied that I wouldn't be in either, as I was friends with both of them.

Both Jason and Paul had been with me a long time and were part of the furniture at SBC, but the events leading up to this fight had driven a wedge through the gym. Everyone was picking sides, which I disliked. An aspect that made me particularly uncomfortable was that Paul was black and Jason was white, which maybe seemed to inform some of the choices made among my members. I didn't feel like we needed that sort of divisive energy. Not at all. One of the great things about boxing is that it always brings black and white kids together.

Bernard was loving all the hullabaloo and attention, walking round like he was Don King. Paul had t-shirts printed with

'100% Silk' on the front. A few kids in the gym started wearing them, so Jason had some t-shirts printed with '100% Bad Boy' on the front and gave them out. Other kids started wearing those. It was all getting more and more tribal.

I told everyone in the gym they could support whoever they liked, as long as they remembered it was just a boxing match. The trainers, on the other hand, had to stay neutral. On the night, there was going to be a winner and a loser, and we would all have to come back to the gym and get along afterwards.

By the night of the weigh-in, things were extremely tense. All Paul's people arrived with their '100% Silk' t-shirts on, standing around being serious, trying to look mean. He had a load of bodybuilders from a gym in Rotherham flanking him, all these massive steroid monsters, which felt a bit unnecessary. Jason, on the other hand, was having a laugh and trying to make light of it all.

The next morning, I was in the gym at 9am as I usually was and once again told the trainers not to wear any t-shirts with the boys' names on.

'We need to be professional,' I said.

That night, Paul turned up to the venue in a limo, with Bernard wearing an all-white suit like something out of *Miami Vice*. He looked an absolute prick. It was a show at a leisure centre that held 800 people, not a world title fight at the MGM Grand. I was cringing so much it hurt.

Jason agreed to enter the ring first, as Bernard had arranged some mad entrance for Paul with scaffolding and God-knows-what. It took ages for Paul to get to the ring and Jason had to wait, which was irritating for everyone. While all this was going on, I noticed one of the amateur trainers from my gym in the corner with Paul, wearing a '100% Silk' t-shirt, which annoyed me.

A couple of fighters noticed it too and approached me saying they didn't want that trainer with them next time they boxed. I was seething. I knew this sort of thing would happen, which is why I told trainers, several times, not to pick a side.

At last, the bell rang and both kids set off at a fast pace. Jason caught Paul early on and it looked like Paul's legs wobbled. But as time wore on, Paul got stronger while Jason slowed until round five when Paul started punching in combination. Jason was done by then, and the referee stopped the bout.

As Jason's cornermen, Andy Manning and Martin Jolley jumped in the ring to help their fighter, Ian Alcock from Paul's corner said something to them. I couldn't hear it but saw the expression on their faces. They did not look happy at all. Worse than that, Paul refused to shake hands with Jason.

I walked towards the changing rooms to wait for Jason to be examined by the doctor, with a heavy heart. I had hoped that once the fight was over, all the bad blood would dissipate, but it didn't seem that was happening.

I put someone on the door to make sure only authorised people could get in the changing rooms and when Jason arrived, he wasn't as upset as I thought he might be. Some of the people around him seemed more agitated. Jason even went into Paul's changing room to try to let Paul know there were no hard feelings. I asked heavyweight Paul King to go with him just to make sure everything was okay.

I was told as they arrived at the changing room door, one of the bodybuilders put his hands on King and asked him what they wanted. This proved to be the starting point of a night of mayhem.

Paul King was not the type of guy to let that pass and that was all made worse because Silky Jones refused to speak to Jason. When Jason came back to his changing room, he was upset and felt disrespected.

One of their trainers came across to try to calm everything down and to see if Jason was okay. As he walked in, Martin Jolley said something to him. He replied and then Martin slapped him across the side of his head. I was trying to calm everyone down as it was all getting very heated. I told Jason to go to the other side of the changing room while we sorted things out. Everyone was sticking their noses in. It was only a matter of time before the changing room exploded.

Meanwhile, a boxer called Paul Owen still had his bandages on from his fight and asked me if I would cut them off. I sat him down on a bench, then got to work.

As I was cutting, I heard someone shout, 'Don't let that cunt come over here!' I looked up to see the SBC trainer from Silky's corner coming through the door, still with his '100% Silk' t-shirt on.

I immediately told him I thought it was a bad idea to go over to where Jason and his mates were, but the trainer started arguing. He kept saying he just wanted to tell Jason there were no hard feelings.

'Look pal, save it for another time,' I told him, but he wouldn't listen. I knew if he went over to where Jason was, there would be trouble.

He started arguing with me. It turned into a full-on row and I had a go at him for wearing the t-shirt. His attitude pissed me off and he wasn't budging, so I ended up hitting him with a left hook. As he went down, he grabbed hold of me, pulling me to the floor. I found myself on top of him, but still had my fingers in the scissors I had been using to cut off Paul Owen's hand-wraps. Someone was screaming to get the scissors, as if I was going to stab him with them, but I wasn't. They just happened to be in my hand.

We were pulled apart and somehow everything calmed enough for us all to go home. I went home that night feeling terrible, which got worse the next day. When I woke up the following morning, Simon Meeks, a reporter from the local newspaper, rang me to get my version of what had happened.

I soon got an inevitable phone call from the Board. Someone had been on the phone to them, hoping to get me in trouble, so I called the trainer that night to apologise. It was the right thing to do, I thought, although he wasn't very gracious about it.

The following night, the local newspaper reported on the show, of which I was also the promoter, with the headline, 'Boxing coaches in punch up!' with an old picture of my face next to it. They chose one, deliberately I guess, in which I was grimacing, to make me look like an absolute nutcase.

Not my finest hour.

24

IT MIGHT sound strange, bearing in mind what happened at Herringthorpe, but other than that, this was a period where things felt settled. I was 40 years old by then. The gym was well established, with a fantastic crowd of fighters, from young amateurs through to the pros and I was beginning to see kids I had trained from an early age embark on careers in the paid ranks, which felt like a real achievement. It's one thing to take on a professional fighter and coach him, but another to start a kid off, teach them the basics, then watch them grow and grow.

Professionally, I began branching out in other ways, too. My interest in boxing history led me to promote 'An Evening with Marvin Hagler' at the Grosvenor House hotel in Sheffield, in association with a contact of mine called Pat Brogan, who arranged for Hagler to come over. When I met the great middleweight champ of the eighties, I was shocked how small he was, and I must admit, despite all my experience in the game, I felt a little starstruck.

That led on to a similar event with the former heavyweight great, Ken Norton, also at the Grosvenor. Predictably, Norton was a huge and imposing man, even though he was nearly 60 years old. When he first shook my hand, I felt like a child. I suspected if he had wanted to, he could have crushed my finger bones in his grip.

After the success of the first two, I began planning an evening with Jake 'Raging Bull' LaMotta, a long-time hero of mine. That one took quite a while to put together, although I had a contact through the gym in Jersey City I had visited. I finally managed to get him over in 2002.

I organised a limo to collect LaMotta from the airport and went to meet him personally. They say 'never meet your heroes', but I don't agree with that advice and was eager to spend some time with him.

To begin with, he fell asleep in the car, but woke up halfway up the M1, asked for a cigarette, then started talking. I had so many questions I wanted to ask and got him chatting about his training methods, his problems making the weight, his attitude to sparring. I just found it so fascinating to be able to pick the brains of someone who occupied such a place in boxing folklore.

Throughout the visit, LaMotta impressed all of us with his stamina. He was in his eighties by this point but took so much time to speak to people and sign autographs. The attention really fired him up and best of all, he was such an interesting speaker.

We did another with the great Roberto Duran, which was also a fantastic experience. I asked Duran about his legendary trainers Freddy Brown and Ray Arcel and was shocked to hear that contrary to popular belief, neither of them were instrumental in his early career. When they did come on the scene, he said Freddy did all the work and Ray would just come to camp for the last two weeks and take all the credit.

Duran was a great sport and very down to earth. He visited my gym and sparred with the kids there, which he didn't have to do. They really enjoyed his visit and it was wonderful to see a legend of the sport prepared to give his time for that.

This was also a time in which there seemed to be a lot of media interest in my gym. I think the legend of Sheffield as Britain's boxing capital had begun to take hold. Brendan had a lot to do with that, of course, but it reflected on all of us. A film producer got in touch and asked if I had ever thought about a fly-on-the-wall documentary. It didn't seem a terrible idea, so that started a little spell where this guy hung around constantly. He kept talking about how amazing the material was, but nothing much came of it and after a while, he seemed to drift away.

By this time, several kids I had trained from the beginning were making great strides, which was exciting to me. In many ways, it was more exciting than going to world title nights with Herol or Richie.

John 'Fireball' Fewkes could really fight, Sam Sheedy was a beautifully balanced boxer with quick hands, while Ross Burkinshaw was another with a lot of promise. They were all seeing lots of action on amateur shows and taking up a great deal of my time. By 2003, Fewkes had reached the finals of the junior ABAs. I had such high hopes for him, and he generated a lot of local buzz.

It's funny as a boxing trainer because you work with these young people in the gym every day. You go to shows with them, celebrate when they win and comfort them when they lose. Some stay in the sport, some drift away, but you end up developing a close bond with them. Hilary used to tell me, not necessarily in the kindest way, that I spent more time with the lads in the gym than I did with my own kids. I had to admit she was right.

Then, at the beginning of 2004, things took an interesting turn when I got a call from Dennis Hobson. I hadn't spoken to Dennis much for a while, but of course I knew that his star fighter Clinton Woods' career had come on leaps and bounds since I last worked with him. Clinton had moved up to light-heavyweight following his loss to David Starie. That interested me as his failure to make super-middleweight for that fight had been blamed on my decision to work with Herol in Miami. It appeared that rather than that, Clinton had simply filled out naturally, as happens to a lot of men in their twenties.

Anyway, it seemed the move up to light-heavyweight had suited him, as by early 2004, he had been European and Commonwealth champion and was a top, world title contender, coming off the back of a loss to all-time great Roy Jones Junior.

After Jones had vacated the world titles to go up to heavyweight, they had fragmented and Clinton had boxed the Jamaican Glen Johnson for the IBF world title, which had been declared a draw.

There had been some fall-out in the camp afterwards, as there so often is, and Clinton's trainer, the former heavyweight world champion, Tim Witherspoon, from America, was sacked. Clinton was scheduled to box a rematch with Johnson at the end of February, was being trained by his old coach, Neil Port, and Dennis asked if I would be happy to tape Clinton's hands before the fight.

I was happy to help as I had been intending to go to the show anyway. It did make me wonder if all was well within Clinton's team, though. Here was a guy boxing for one of the four major world titles in a week's time, but there was no one working in his camp who could wrap hands. It didn't suggest a very professional set-up.

I arrived at the venue before Clinton that night and bumped into Paul 'Silky' Jones, which could have been awkward, as it was the first time I had seen him since the mental night at Herringthorpe. Fortunately, he was ready to put the unpleasantness behind him. We shook hands, had a chat and even arranged to meet for a cup of tea the following week. That was a relief, at least. Paul and I had a long history, stretching all the way back to our time at Brendan's together and it's never nice when you feel an old friend has become an enemy. With that put to bed, I headed backstage and found Clinton's dressing room.

Clinton seemed tense and nervy when he arrived, so I did my best to settle him down even though that wasn't really my job. We had a nice conversation as I wrapped his hands and just like with Paul Jones before, it was great to reconnect with him and see that there were no hard feelings. I had never felt that Clinton had necessarily wanted to sack me as his trainer anyway. The situation had purely been created by the impossible choice I was forced to make, then his team reacting to the fall-out. Clinton and I hugged before I left, and I wished him all the best. No matter what had happened in the past, he was definitely a kid I wanted to do well.

Once the action started, as I watched from ringside, I thought Clinton fought the wrong fight. Johnson was throwing big right hands over the top that nearly always landed and if I am honest, I didn't think Clinton's corner did a good job. In fact, I felt sorry for the kid. When he came back between rounds, they were verbally beating him up and he didn't look like he needed that, at all. I felt some help and encouragement were required. Clinton was clearly struggling. As usual he showed plenty of courage but after 12 rounds there was only one winner.

Afterwards the changing room was quiet, as it always is in this situation. There were a few people standing around, but no one was speaking much and, as I walked in, people just shrugged their shoulders.

'I've never been hit so hard,' Clinton said. He was slumped on a bench at the side of the room. 'Not even Roy Jones hit me that hard.'

Meanwhile, Dennis Hobson was putting his tie on and Neil Port, the trainer, sat by himself looking fed up at the other side of the room. Clinton's dad said to me, 'I'm glad his mother weren't here to see it.'

Clinton had taken a lot of heavy shots, seemed a little dazed and was struggling to put his trousers on. I told him to sit down and relax. There was no rush to leave the building. I dragged over a massage table and Clinton climbed on it. I asked Clinton if the doctor had been to see him yet.

'I don't think so,' Clinton said. 'But I've got a really bad headache.'

I began to feel worried for him. He hadn't seemed right before the fight and certainly didn't seem right after it, so I said I would go and fetch a doctor.

I walked straight to ringside and told Simon Block from the British Boxing Board of Control that someone had better get a doctor to check on Clinton. Block could see on my face that I was worried, and immediately got one of the ringside doctors to go backstage.

The doc examined Clinton, diagnosed a concussion, then asked Clinton how he was getting home. He warned Clinton's wife that if the symptoms got worse or he started vomiting, he would need to go straight to hospital.

'I've never been hit so hard,' Clinton kept saying. 'Never been hit so hard. He even hurt me to the body. He hit me so hard.'

It was upsetting to see him like that and it preyed on my mind for days afterwards. I kept thinking of Michael Watson who by then was learning to walk again, or worse, Bradley Stone. It would have been devastating if anything had happened to Clinton.

I waited a few days, then phoned him. He told me it had been a difficult training camp.

'I could tell,' I replied.

More than anything, I was just pleased he sounded well.

25

SBC'S MAIN heavyweight at the time was a kid called Paul King. He was originally from Parson Cross ABC and was a decent, tough kid, without being a world beater. Paul was three fights into his pro career, when I got a call from John Ingle, Brendan's son, asking if I would be interested in Paul fighting their heavyweight, Carl Baker. According to Brendan, Baker was the next off the St Thomas' conveyor belt and was a future heavyweight champion of the world.

My initial concern was that Paul weighed 16 stone and Carl weighed 22. It often works that way with the heavies but that's a lot of weight to give away. I spoke to Paul though and he was very confident, saying he had beaten Baker in the amateurs. Nonetheless, there was a part of me that didn't want the aggro. Things seemed to have calmed down since the Johnny Nelson fiasco and I didn't want more SBC v Ingle gym nonsense, but boxing is boxing. I called John Ingle back and told him the fight was on. Obviously, it was an Ingle promotion, and we were in the away corner.

Paul didn't train very hard, as was his habit, and I was perhaps too soft on him. I always struggled to berate fighters for not doing enough strength and conditioning work, because that's exactly what I had been like, myself. He kept repeating that he knew he would beat him, so I let things take their natural course.

Of course, *Boxing News* picked Baker, the new Ingle star, to win and I began to suspect they were probably right. Paul seemed so unmotivated beforehand and could barely be bothered to warm up in the dressing room.

As we headed for the ring, I noticed Ryan Rhodes standing near our corner.

'Hi, Glyn,' he said, with a smile. I smiled back and again, it was nice to feel that the wounds were healing. We didn't always have to be at each other's throats, did we?

We waited in the ring until Brendan started walking in with Baker and once they climbed in, I found myself facing Brendan across the canvas for the very first time.

The fighters were called to centre ring by the ref, to give his instructions. Brendan and I followed. There we were, face to face.

I offered my hand to Brendan. He took it, but there was something a little strange in that handshake. This was a man who had patted me on the back or nudged me or given me a playful whack many times, yet this was our first physical contact for so very long. Despite everything, deep inside myself, I still had such a lot of affection for Brendan, and it welled up inside me right then, but that certainly wasn't the time to express it.

It wasn't a great fight, in truth. Baker lumbered after Paul, but he was such a huge lump and ran out of gas after a couple of rounds. After that it was like watching Paul hitting the heavy bag. He kept jabbing and moving his feet and picked up an easy points win.

Of course, we celebrated like mad. Underdog victories are always the sweetest. I caught Brendan staring daggers at me from across the ring. His exciting new heavyweight prospect wasn't so exciting anymore and it was all our fault. Clearly, it wasn't time for a reconciliation just yet.

Although Brendan and I had missed the opportunity to kiss and make up, despite a thawing of the frost between us, there was still time to reconnect with old friends. Two months after Paul King upset the odds against Carl Baker, Richie Wenton turned up at my house.

'Alright, Glyn?' he asked. 'Can you do me a favour?'

'Don't agree to train him,' a voice said in the back of my mind. *'Don't agree to train him. Don't agree to train him.'*

Fortunately, Richie wasn't mad enough to be making a comeback. He asked if I would help him lay a wooden floor in his new house that was across the road from my place.

Of course, I agreed, and as we worked, we talked about days gone by. We both had some negative feelings we had to work through. I told Richie how annoyed I was when he did the interview in the local paper saying how great training with Brendan was. He laughed it off and came back at me with a few of his own comments. It was good to clear the air.

While shaking Brendan's hand and shooting the breeze with Richie helped me feel better about the past, there was still plenty going on in the here and now. John Fewkes turned 19 and I had a chat with him, suggesting his time had come to turn pro. He had been with me since he was 11 years old, had boxed almost 60 amateur bouts, represented England and reached the finals of the ABAs. Alongside his amateur pedigree I really felt his style would suit the pros, especially his vicious body punching.

I wanted the best for John, so reached out to a few people around the scene and ended up striking a deal with the Scottish promoter Tommy Gilmore. We would co-manage John to secure the best opportunities possible for him. A meeting was soon held with Dennis Hobson, who was promoting a show at the Don Valley Stadium. He offered John a place on the show without signing a contract, which suited us. In other words, John could box on Dennis' show with no further obligations at all.

As the show neared, I got more and more anxious, often finding myself unable to sleep. I really wanted things to work out for John. He had worked hard and sold 250 tickets, which was good going, but there had been issues finding him an opponent.

The night before the fight I was phoned by Richard Poxon, who had become Dennis Hobson's right-hand man, and was told they had lined up 35-year-old Karl Taylor. He outweighed Fewkes by half a stone and had been a good fighter in his day. I thought it was too risky.

I explained this to Poxon in no uncertain terms and he started panicking. For the next couple of hours, he rang me constantly with different opponents. None of them were any good.

Things got worse when Poxon called me back for the umpteenth time to say that there was still no opponent and now they were worried because Kell Brook (from the Ingle gym) was fighting on the same bill. The majority of the Fireball's tickets had been sold to Sheffield Wednesday fans, while most of Brook's crowd supported Sheffield United. As a result, someone had told Dennis there was likely to be trouble at the show. Finally, though, Poxon came up with a suggestion that was more acceptable than the others and I gave him the thumbs-up.

John boxed really well, hurt his opponent and forced a second-round stoppage, triggering the usual post-fight celebrations at a nightclub. You never know what you are going to get when a boxer is starting out but there was a lot of expectation around Fewkes. I felt, as someone who had seen all levels of the sport, from world title class down, that if things went his way, he could really make his mark.

From there, things continued moving along for a few years, as they do. By early 2009, John had a record of 16 wins from 16 fights and was preparing to step into title class. Meanwhile, Sam Sheedy had turned pro and won his first couple. Ross Burkinshaw had a handful of pro fights under his belt, and I had some great kids coming through the junior sessions too.

We then received a visit from none other than Clinton Woods. Since the last time I had worked with him, wrapping his hands before he lost a gruelling bout for the IBF world title, he had made another comeback, won that title, then defended it four times. That put Clinton right up there with some of the biggest names in British boxing. There were not many world champions from the UK at that time.

In April 2008, he had lost his world title to the American Antonio Tarver after a whole string of problems in his camp. I had been there for the fight out in Florida and went to see Clinton in the changing room afterwards. He was absolutely devastated. After that night, the team around him crumbled and Clinton retired for the third or fourth time. He had a period away from the ring, then decided he wanted one last crack.

'Will you train me?' he asked.

'Of course I will, mate,' I replied. And suddenly I was working with someone at the very top end of the game again.

26

THERE WERE no tune-ups after Clinton's lay-off. Dennis Hobson lined up a world title eliminator against the Kosovan Elivir Muriqi in Jersey. The winner would be in pole position to box the champion in their next fight.

Obviously, I had worked with a world-class fighter on the comeback trail before, in the form of Herol Graham. This comeback felt different and didn't seem as ill-advised to me. Clinton was still right up there and there was no reason at all to believe he couldn't beat Muriqi. If he did, then who knew what could happen?

Clinton trained hard at home, before we flew out to Jersey for a week before the fight to finish off. We stayed in a lovely hotel along with the other fighters on the bill and their teams. One morning at breakfast, I introduced myself to Muriqi's trainer, then sat and interrogated him for a while. He didn't know who I was, and I think he thought I was just a boxing fan. He talked and talked, and among other things, he told me that Buddy McGirt, the famous American coach, was flying over from America to work Muriqi's corner. Later in the day, the same guy saw me in the lobby with Clinton, realised who I was and started shouting abuse at me. We just laughed at him. Round one to us.

Overall, it wasn't an especially happy camp, though. There was an awful atmosphere between Clinton, Richard Poxon and Dennis Hobson. Poxon had trained Clinton for his previous few fights, but Clinton sacked him after the Tarver loss. However, because Poxon was so heavily involved in Hobson's affairs, he was still lurking in the background.

What Richard seemed to forget, from my point of view, was that he had been very fortunate to have trained Clinton in the first place. Most trainers have a boxing background but Richard started at my gym as a keep-fitter. He had never boxed or had any real experience in the sport, then somehow found himself training a world-class fighter. He had just been in the right place at the right time.

His childish behaviour in Jersey, whenever Clinton was near him, was pathetic. I told the security team to make sure Clinton did not set eyes on Richard, especially on fight night. Poxon made it so clear to everyone that he wished Clinton the worst, and we didn't need those sorts of bad vibes in the air.

As the time for the weigh-in neared, I began to have some small concerns about Clinton. His weight was fine, and he was injury-free, which was important, as the build-up to his loss against Tarver had been impaired by all sorts of physical problems. There just seemed to be so much nonsense around him though, with his management and former team. Part of me wondered how much Clinton had left in the tank at 36. Did he still really want this?

He had always been a quiet, self-doubting type of kid, so what I really had to do was get inside Clinton's head and make him believe in himself. He had to believe he could still do it. We spent a lot of time talking that week.

We all went out for a big meal after the weigh-in. Clinton had a couple of close friends out with him, and everyone seemed relaxed. He had faced Muriqi down without trouble, had looked much bigger than him and had said something to him, on stage, out of earshot of everyone else, which looked as though it rattled him. I was pleased with how things had gone.

After the meal, we went for a long walk and just talked. Matt Mowatt arrived in Jersey to work the corner with me, and once Clinton went to bed, we sat around and talked for hours. Perhaps that was me showing my nerves.

I had known Clinton a long time. As a trainer, you always feel such a great responsibility because that fighter has trusted you to prepare them for what can be a life-or-death situation. Clinton had a lot riding on this fight, and it was important for me to talk it out.

Fight day passed off smoothly and Clinton seemed nice and calm beforehand, cracking jokes in the dressing room, but the mood was spoiled when he needed a last-minute toilet visit before walking to the ring. I took him down the corridor to the bathroom and of course, we bumped into Poxon. Clinton and Richard actually physically bumped into each other as they passed and the antagonism in the encounter was tangible. Neither of them spoke but they exchanged a horrible look and I feared for what this had done to Clinton's mental state.

On the night, Clinton began very strongly. As usual I shouted abuse at Muriqi every time the two boxers were near our corner, anything I could think of to put him off.

By the halfway stage, Clinton was well on top and Muriqi resorted to chucking low blows so, as the seventh round ended, I jumped into the ring and followed Muriqi back to his corner, talking rubbish in his ear. The ref, Howard Foster, grabbed me and gave me a telling-off. He said if I did that again he would deduct a point from Clinton, which didn't bother me. The important thing was I had achieved my aim and got into Muriqi's head. He kept looking over between rounds, scowling at me. I knew I had taken his mind off the job in hand.

Towards the end of the fight, Clinton even looked as though he might force a stoppage. Muriqi was tough, though. I had to credit him for that.

Of course, when Clinton was announced as a clear points winner, celebrations kicked in and all the way back to the changing room, I was slapped on the back and told how well I had done, that Clinton hadn't boxed so well for years and all the rest of it. It was well-intentioned and I enjoyed it, but I also knew very well not to get too high on it. These would be the same people who would be berating me if Clinton had lost. It's important, as a trainer, not to get too ahead of yourself when things go your way and not to get too down when they don't. The truth is that it's never fully down to you either way, so a sense of perspective is important.

As I always did, I went into Muriqi's room and shook hands with him. I told him I didn't really mean the things I had been shouting during the fight and he hugged me and said, 'No hard feelings.' Buddy McGirt was pretty dismissive, though. He didn't seem like he had handled the defeat very well, so I left him to it. Life's too short to deal with bad losers.

While Clinton unwound at the after-party, Matt and I chatted about possibilities for the future. Tarver was set to box Chad Dawson for the IBF world title and Clinton's win meant he was in line to fight the winner. That most likely meant a high-profile, American show, again. Once more, it seemed that I had a world title fight on the horizon.

After returning home, it was straight back to the meat-and-potatoes side of boxing, as I was set to promote another show at the Grosvenor Hotel in Sheffield. A whole bunch of kids from my gym were on the card, including Sam 'Speedy' Sheedy, who was turning into a very useful southpaw, although he wasn't the strongest kid, mentally. He was someone who needed a lot of looking after, to make the most of his physical gifts and didn't seem to relish fighting, as some kids do. We also had Jason Carr, Monsoor Wali, Danny Tombs, and a light-heavyweight kid who I had a lot of time for, called Carl Wild. Carl was the opposite of Sam in some ways. He was never likely to be a champion but was game as they come and loved to fight.

The usual headaches with ticket sales ensued. Compared to 25 years earlier when I was fighting, small hall boxing had ceased to have much of a casual, walk-up audience, meaning the only way to make it work financially was for fighters to personally sell enough tickets to cover costs. All the lads on the bill promised to do their bit so I wouldn't be out of pocket. Like a mug, I believed them.

The week before the show I told all the boxers I needed the money in before the show on the Sunday.

'Yes, Glyn. No problem, Glyn. Of course, Glyn.'

On Saturday, I was in the gym at nine. Carl came in first, looking a bit guilty. He said he'd only shifted 55 tickets because a load of his mates let him down. One by one, the other lads all arrived with similar stories. Not one of them had sold enough tickets to cover themselves, meaning I was looking at a hefty loss on the show. This is the reality of modern boxing promotion and while I felt for the lads, it was still irritating. Punting out tickets to friends and family isn't easy, but you have to do it, or the show loses money. If every show lost money, then lower-level boxing would cease to exist. That would be no good for anyone.

Everyone boxed well on the night and picked up wins apart from Carl, topping the bill in his hometown. He had a tough night, took some punishment and was given a draw.

As I was about to leave the venue, one of the whips shouted to me that he had discovered a problem. Apparently, the kid who boxed Carl Wild hadn't worn the correct gloves.

'What did he wear, then?' I asked.

'He brought his own,' the whip said. 'Mexican gloves, Cleto Reyes.'

'What?'

Incensed, I walked towards the changing rooms and got there just as Carl's opponent was coming out of the door.

'Hello, pal,' I said. 'So, you wore your own gloves today, did you?'

'Yes,' he said, innocently. 'I always do.'

I walked into the changing room and his team were all standing around, including his manager.

'Oi,' I said. 'Your kid just boxed my kid in his own gloves.'

'What's wrong with that?' one of them asked.

What a bunch of muppets. They knew the rules as well as I did. I shook my head.

'You've all been around long enough to know you can't bring your own gloves. Besides, Reyes are punchers' gloves, which is why my kid's face is all bashed up. You're well out of order. My fighter's boxing in big BBE gloves and your boy's in those? It's a piss-take.'

'Well, what are you gonna do?' the manager asked. 'Make a complaint or forget about it?'

That really annoyed me. This was a guy who had never been punched in the face with a glove in his life, which is why he could take it so lightly.

An official report was submitted to the area council, by the inspector at the show, and I was informed that both the trainer and the fighter would be called to appear, to explain why they fought in their own gloves.

A few weeks later, I had Carl Wild boxing again, in Bolton and as luck would have it, the same trainer was there at the show, with another fighter. As soon as we got settled in, he came bowling over as if he had a score to settle.

'You've got me in some right fucking trouble,' he said.

I took a step back. 'No,' I replied. 'You got yourself in some right fucking trouble.'

He put his arm round my waist as if he wanted to drag me away, so I turned and got ready to throw a right hand, like a cowboy drawing his gun.

'Please,' he said. 'Can't we sort it out here? My man's got to miss a day of work to appear at the area council meeting. Can't we just forget it?'

I shook my head and walked away.

When the meeting rolled around, the inspector's letter was read out and an official who had been an inspector on the show said he would leave the room, because his involvement in the show meant he couldn't stay in the meeting, as per the rules. That obviously gave the other trainer ideas and he pointed at me, shouting that I shouldn't be allowed in the meeting either, as I had promoted the show.

The chairman interjected and said I should be allowed to stay because the report came from the inspector and not me. From there, it all turned into a comedy sketch. The chairman told me to sit back down, so I did. Then someone else said it wasn't fair if I was present. So, I shrugged and stood back up.

The trainer of the kid with dodgy gloves then started ranting on, going red in the face. John Ingle whispered to me that the bloke looked like he was going to have a heart attack, at which the trainer got really upset. I began walking to the door, but was told to sit down again. The other trainer started having a go at me, so I called him a dickhead and the chairman shouted for everyone to be quiet. This is the very orderly and mature world of professional boxing.

The chairman told the council that I was allowed to stay in the room but wouldn't be allowed to vote on any decision. At that point, none other than Brendan Ingle piped up.

'I think Glyn Rhodes should be sent out of the room,' he said. In my imagination it felt like he looked at me and said, *'you tick bastard'* just as he always used to do. Fortunately, the chairman ignored him.

A long discussion about gloves ensued, with the result that the other trainer and boxer were fined £1,000. Naturally this upset him hugely and he left the meeting swearing his revenge.

'Wonderful,' I thought as I drove home. 'Just what I need, another enemy.'

27

BY JUNE of 2009, Clinton Woods was back in training for another tilt at the IBF light-heavyweight championship of the world. The title picture at the top of the division had got messy, as it so often does in modern boxing. He wasn't due to fight Tarver or Dawson as we had expected, but a new kid on the block called Tavoris Cloud in Florida in August. The title had been vacated, so the IBF had ordered the number one and two contenders to box for it.

By this point, as I approached 50 years of age, I had been swimming around like mad in the boxing goldfish bowl for pretty much my whole life. I had allowed it to consume me, to a large degree, mainly by necessity. Boxing had been good to me and dragged me out of my council estate roots. But it also took a lot, too.

Every day I was in the gym, constantly busy with my stable of fighters. If I wasn't with my fighters, I was thinking about them. Rather than a job, boxing was a 24/7 obsession, and in some ways, that's not healthy.

Unlike friends of mine who worked set hours and had weekends off, I never had downtime. Nearly every Friday or Saturday evening I was at a boxing show somewhere and often Sundays too. That meant Hilary and the kids found themselves left to their own devices. When 'normal' families might have been going out on day trips or eating meals together, ours didn't do those things. It's not that that's how I wanted things to be. I genuinely loved Hilary and the kids. It was just that my life hadn't played out in that way.

With that in mind, I should perhaps have been a bit wiser, maybe read the room a little better, but no. On a Sunday afternoon, Hilary asked to speak to me in the kitchen. As usual I was rushing about.

'What do you want?' I asked her.

'Glyn,' she said. I got a lump in my throat. I could tell by her face this wasn't going to be good. 'I don't love you anymore.'

There was something chilling in the way she said it, cold and businesslike, so serious. She said she had been thinking about it for some time but had wanted to be sure. I felt like she had reached down my throat and tied my guts in a massive knot.

The conversation left me devastated and feeling dizzy. Hilary had been resolute. She had made up her mind. Fifteen years of togetherness were over, and we began the painful process of separating.

Fortunately, Clinton's upcoming title fight gave me something else to think about. I had to get my act together for his sake and I did so by telling myself that there are people who spend a lifetime in boxing, but never get the chance to do what I was about to do. I needed to appreciate the opportunity but in truth all I really wanted was to be back at home with my family. You never truly know what you have until you lose it.

I made a conscious effort to keep my personal problems away from Clinton in the build-up to his fight. We trained in Sheffield for a while, then flew out to Florida where we used a gym just across from the hotel. Clinton's head seemed in a good place, and he was doing well physically, especially for a 37-year-old who had built up a fair bit of wear and tear over the years.

I was asked to say a few words at the press conference, and told the crowd that Clinton was fit and a great professional, that his opponent was in for a tough fight. I kept it low-key on purpose, and I didn't want to come out with all the usual lines about best shape of his life, best training camp ever and so on. That's not my style.

Clinton spoke very well too although he's not a bloke who talks much in day-to-day life. Once upon a time, he would have struggled with this sort of situation, but he was seasoned to it by then. As I listened to him, I thought about how this was another side of boxing that people don't consider. It wasn't just a sport which taught balance, punching technique and defence, but also self-confidence and soft skills like communication. He managed the whole thing without bluster or silliness and the audience seemed very appreciative.

There was time for a brief altercation with one of Cloud's team when the gloves came out before the fight. This sort of thing was bread and butter to me by then. One guy stood up and started insisting that it was their right to choose the gloves first. I told him to calm down, so he got in my face and started saying he had done time in prison, as if that was going to scare me. I just laughed at him. The two pairs of gloves were identical anyway, so the whole thing was absurd.

Matt arrived from England to help in the corner and by the time we headed to the ring with Clinton and Dennis Hobson, there was a feeling of finality. We all knew that this was Clinton's last hurrah. He had been Dennis' golden boy for years by that point, but even if he won the fight and recaptured the world title, age was catching up with him.

The fight started just as I thought it would. Cloud came out fast, but Clinton had seen it all before, stayed calm and picked the American off with his jab. He was probably edging it on points, but then, from the eighth round, things started to change. It was a classic case of age against youth and when Cloud applied more pressure in the later rounds, Clinton began to tire.

In the tenth and eleventh, Clinton took a few big shots and I started to fear for him. Losing was one thing, but the worst possible outcome would be for him to get badly hurt. Before the 12th, I reckoned he was several rounds down on the cards, and I knew his only chance was to go all out for a stoppage.

'Just keep your hands up,' I told him. 'Just keep your hands up and box. Don't do anything silly and we can all go home.'

He listened and I was so immensely proud of him. He was wise to end his career the right way and not risk everything for machismo. Not many in boxing can do that.

Cloud took the decision, but we left the ring without too much disappointment. Clinton got a lot of plaudits from a crowd that had begun by booing him. It didn't seem such a terrible end to a brilliant career. Clinton Woods could walk away knowing he had been one of Sheffield's (and Britain's) very best.

Back in the changing room I told Clinton to hold his head up because he had achieved so much. He thanked me and I left him to chat with his wife.

The journey home from Florida was not a good one. I knew I was coming back to deal with lots of shit due to my split from Hilary. The excitement of another world title fight was over and I had to return to the wreckage of my personal life and everything which went with it. I believe that's what is known as a reality crash.

I had to get our home valued, with the idea I would either give Hilary half of the value, or move out and sell the house, so both of us could start again. I knew I would struggle to get a mortgage at 49 years old, so settled on the first option. That meant I had to find the money to buy Hilary out.

I was very lucky and managed to borrow some from my mum, stepdad and a few friends. This was better for everyone and meant the kids could stay in the same school.

Although I had managed to keep the house, I was an emotional wreck. Things between me and Hilary were still complicated, and I struggled with the new routine. For example, when I had to collect the kids from school at 3.30pm, it clashed with my gym opening time. The kids coped well and had to start travelling on the bus sometimes, but it was all such a headache. On top of the stresses that came with managing my fighters, I really didn't need it.

This was perhaps the first time in my life that I struggled with mental health, although I wouldn't have thought of it in those terms back then. I generally had a sense of living in a kind of fog and didn't know what I was doing from one minute to the next. Everything seemed stressful and difficult. There were days in the gym when I would just run out of the door. People knew what I was going through and stood by me, but the whole situation definitely took its toll.

Things carried on like that for around a year and at the end of it, I felt like I had aged about ten. People told me there was light at the end of the tunnel, but I couldn't see any fucking light. In the end, I adjusted. I suppose you have to.

28

CLINTON'S RETIREMENT meant I was once again without any world-level pros in the gym, but by this time, a number of my lads were doing really well. Sam Sheedy continued picking up good wins, Carl Wild put up a great display against former world champion Enzo Maccarinelli but was on the wrong end of a soft stoppage in the last round. Ross Burkinshaw won the English title, although things turned sour between us and he left to train at Ryan Rhodes' new gym, which was a terrible shame. Tommy Frank, a great kid, who I had trained from seven years old, won the Yorkshire amateur championship. Tommy was such a battler and had first come to me after recovering from an operation on a hole in his heart. He had been desperately ill as a child and boxing was a way to gain some fitness. The lad had unbelievable spirit.

John Fewkes was still progressing too, although his career hadn't quite taken off in the way we'd all hoped. He got stopped in the fourth round when challenging for the English title and seemed a little lacking in motivation. This is a very common story in boxing. Someone can have plenty of ability, but without the right mindset they won't go too far. It was a story I knew extremely well, as it had been my own story as a boxer many years before.

All of these careers continued on their own trajectories, along with plenty of others, too, and by 2013, a new kid called Scott Westgarth was set to make his debut. He had come to boxing late but was very dedicated and determined to do something in the game. You had to love that. His father had been a fighter and boxed some big names, so he came from good boxing stock.

Scott was an honest trier, with a wonderful sense of humour, who I liked as soon as I met him. He actually ended up losing his first fight on points, mainly through nerves, but was straight back in the gym the next day, eager to put things right. There was something heartwarming about it. He may not have been the most gifted kid, and had a lot to learn, but he had the attitude of a champion.

That's the thing about running a thriving boxing gym. People constantly come and go. You get your heart broken so many times that it becomes a regular part of life. You work with kids for years and then someone gets in their ear, offers them the world and they leave you. On the other hand, the door is always opening, and you never know who is going to walk in. It could be some 50-year-old headcase who did a bit of boxing three decades back and wants to lose weight, a parent bringing their timid son or daughter for the first time, or someone who's looking to train seriously and box on shows.

Around the same time as Scott made his debut in 2013, that gym door opened, and two African guys walked in. One had a mohawk hairstyle, like Mr T in *Rocky III*. The other one introduced himself as a pastor and said he had come along to help the mohawk guy, who was a friend of his. The mohawk fellow couldn't speak much English but was a boxer looking to turn professional. So, we had a chat.

It turned out this kid had arrived in my doorway with one hell of a backstory. He was called Serge Ambomo and had boxed for Cameroon in the 2012 Olympics in London. After getting eliminated from the tournament, he and seven of his team-mates disappeared from the Olympic Village and claimed asylum to stay in the UK. For some reason, he made his way up to Sheffield and came to see me.

I took Serge on. He was good in the gym and incredibly strong for a welterweight, although also crude. It was difficult to know how far he could go, but I was sure he could be a handful for anyone.

He made his debut in September 2013 on one of my shows at the Concord Centre. There was a lot of interest in Serge because of his history, so we had plenty of media coverage and found ourselves doing tons of interviews, which is unusual for a small hall event.

Serge looked the business that night and I wondered if I might have someone a bit special on my hands. He was so cool walking to the ring, like he was made for it. He boxed a journeyman called Matt Seawright and I could tell, within about 20 seconds of watching from the corner, that Serge was way too strong for him. At the end of the first round, I told him to ease up. I wanted him to get some rounds in rather than force a stoppage. He listened to me, which I liked, and won an easy points decision after four rounds of one-sided action. Ambomo had something about him, a bit of attitude and I wondered if it would make him stand out from the crowd.

It was a good night for us overall. Sam Sheedy boxed superbly in the main event to record his 12th straight win against a tough opponent. There had been some changes at the gym, but things still looked positive.

Alongside all the work with amateur and professional fighters, more than anything, I was proud of what SBC had come to represent. By this time, hundreds of young kids had trained with me, many of them from troubled backgrounds after growing up on some of Sheffield's toughest estates. We took them away on training camps and provided something positive in lives that lacked it. We had also been involved in several charity events and raised somewhere in the region of £350,000. To me, this encapsulated what a boxing gym was supposed to be all about. It wasn't just a place to prepare for boxing matches, it was a community resource and a refuge for those who needed it.

I had never done all that stuff to seek recognition, but to my huge surprise, this side of my work had not gone unnoticed. We were approaching Christmas, and life had settled down again following all the trauma of my split from Hilary. I was standing in the kitchen with my kids Joseph and Jorja, my mum and my stepdad, when there was a knock on the door. It was our next-door neighbour Mick, who had taken delivery of a recorded letter for me while I had been out.

I invited Mick in, opened the large brown envelope and started to read it. Quickly, this turned into one of those moments in which time stood still. A sense of unreality washed over me, while my family and neighbour stared at me, quizzically. Unusually, I was lost for words, so Joseph stepped forward and took the letter from my hand.

'Bloody hell,' he said, and showed it around.

I had been awarded the MBE in the Queen's New Year's honours list for services to boxing and the community.

The letter explained that this could not become public knowledge before the honours list was formally announced, so everyone in the kitchen had to swear a vow of silence.

By March of the following year, we were allowed to discuss it publicly and a party was arranged to celebrate my MBE at the prestigious Cutlers' Hall just outside Sheffield. We sold all the tickets, which was lovely and many friends from throughout my life were set to attend, even people from Brendan's gym, so the whole thing gave me a nice feeling.

It was a fantastic night with hundreds of people in attendance. When the MC called me out, I felt nervous, as if I was walking out for a fight. My kids were with me and Joseph looked frightened too, but Jorja was icy cool. I felt like crying as we walked to our seats with everyone clapping, but managed to hold it in.

What was particularly special was that so many lads I had trained stood up to say a few words. John Fewkes, Reagan Denton, Ross Burkinshaw, Carl Wild, Lee Edwards and a few more. It choked me up and reignited lots of memories.

Soon after that wonderful evening, Serge Ambomo had his second contest down at York Hall. He trained extremely hard for it and arrived looking like he was carved out of stone. Serge boxed a local kid called Adam Salman and tore him to pieces, stopping him in the fourth round.

That was all well and good, but Serge didn't perhaps understand the tribalism of British boxing, where a lot of fans bring football-style attitudes to the fights. Of course, the local crowd booed him, which is normal here, but in response, he walked over to the edge of the ring and made a throat-cutting gesture with his glove. The crowd were incensed by that, and I thought for a moment there would be a riot.

Coins and other objects were flying into the ring. I pulled Serge away.

'Are you fucking crazy?' I shouted. He looked at me flatly.

Once we were back in the changing room, I told Serge that we needed to wait for a while until the audience had gone home. Our car was parked close by and the last thing we needed was to meet a mobbed-up bunch of Adam Salman supporters out on the street.

I hoped that Serge had learned his lesson because what I had seen concerned me. Boxing, as I knew only too well, is a dangerous sport and we don't need victorious fighters making gestures like that, especially while their opponent is still being checked to make sure they are okay. Serge might have been from Cameroon, but if he was going to make a career here, he needed to adapt to the British way of doing things. Otherwise, I could see trouble for him ahead.

29

BEFORE LONG, I got a call from Dave Coldwell, who by this time was a trainer, manager and promoter, enquiring about Ambomo. There was quite a lot of buzz about Serge at this time, after his dramatic defection from the athletes' village, the impressiveness of his first two wins and the scene he had caused down at York Hall.

I hadn't had much to do with Coldwell since all the silly business with Johnny Nelson years before, but he asked if I would be happy for Serge to box his fighter, Jerome Wilson, on a show he was promoting, at a new venue called Ice Sheffield.

I must admit, I was a little shocked that he would ask for this fight. Jerome Wilson was a decent talent, with lovely, fast hands, but was still developing. It didn't make a great deal of sense to put him in with a brute like Serge. Serge only really boxed one way and we all knew he would go in there and try to nail Jerome to the floor. Most promoter/managers would steer well clear of putting one of their early career prospects in with someone like that.

I asked Coldwell why he wanted such a tough fight for his kid. He told me he wanted to test his fighter, to see if he had what it takes. He explained that Wilson wasn't a ticket seller, so he was losing money on him and if he didn't come through this, he wouldn't waste any more time with him. This struck me as pretty harsh, but I agreed to take the fight. Serge was one of those guys who was happy to box anybody, and I fancied him to get the win. Wilson was a very tidy boxer, but I reckoned Serge would just walk through him.

On the night, the atmosphere was unbelievable. The contest had been built up locally as a battle of Sheffield and there was quite a bit of needle in the air. The fight was exactly as we expected. Wilson boxed on the move, trying to keep Serge off, but it was a hard job as Serge ploughed forward relentlessly.

It soon turned into an absolutely titanic battle. A great fight to watch but maybe not such a great fight to be involved in. Fights like those can ruin boxers.

Both fighters took counts, although Serge's was just a flash knockdown whereas Wilson was wilting by the time Serge floored him in the third. As the bell rang to end the fight, I thought Serge had done enough, but boxing a Coldwell fighter on a Coldwell show, I wasn't holding my breath.

Surprisingly Serge won a deserved decision to go to 3-0. There was pandemonium in the hall and afterwards, the fight caused a great deal of discussion. Everyone in Sheffield was talking about it and it was spoken about on Sky Sports as being one of the UK's best fights of the year.

Serge really enjoyed the attention. There was also no question that he had made an impressive start to his professional career. I had the feeling that if he could keep his wilder instincts in check, he could go on to win titles. It was tough on Wilson, whose career looked to be on the skids, but Coldwell had known the risks before taking the fight. That's boxing, and what can happen if a fighter isn't being managed by someone looking after their best interests.

A month or two after that I went down to London again, this time with my family, a posh suit and a stomach full of nerves, to receive my MBE. It was an incredible occasion, and I was so happy to share it with my kids, including Alex, my son from my first marriage, although I rarely saw him.

The whole thing reminded me of going away for world title contests with Herol, Richie and Clinton. We stayed in a hotel near Buckingham Palace, so we could walk there the next day. It was a beautiful summer's morning, so perfect that the whole thing almost felt fake, like we were acting in a film. Once we got inside, the scene was incredibly impressive. The décor and wall hangings in the palace were all immaculate. Palace guards stood on the stairs, either side of the red carpet for us to walk on.

Once we reached the top, recipients had to go right, and guests to the left. I waved to my kids and, I must admit, started to feel very alone.

I headed into the room where the presentations would be made and was informed that the Queen had gone to hospital to visit Prince Philip, who was unwell. As a result, Prince Charles would be doing the presentations.

There were hundreds of people waiting and it seemed to take forever for my name to be called, which only served to allow the nerves to build even more. As I headed towards the presentation area, I was amazed to hear a piece of music playing in the background that I knew very well. The *intermezzo* of 'Cavalleria Rusticana' by Pietro Mascagni, the theme music to the movie *Raging Bull* about Jake LaMotta. It sent shivers down my spine.

As I was about to step forwards, I felt faint again and took a big, deep breath to control myself. Suddenly, it was announced over the speaker.

'Glyn Rhodes for services to boxing and the community.'

I walked towards the smiling prince, who shook my hand.

'It's really great what you're doing with the boxing nowadays,' he said.

I didn't have a clue what he was on about, in truth. My head was spinning. I told him we had met before in Sheffield at my gym. I could tell he didn't remember me, although he remembered coming to Burton Street.

He laughed and said, 'That's a long time ago now.'

He pinned the medal on me. I bowed as I was supposed to, and as I walked away, I felt incredibly relieved. Beforehand I was sure I would do something to mess it all up, like trip over my feet, or fart as I was approaching, but none of that happened.

There was a form to sign and a media interview, before I was reunited with my kids and we returned to the main room, where a brass band on the balcony played 'God Save the Queen'.

When the band finished, we headed outside and wandered around the courtyard for a while. There were crowds beyond the fence and out of the blue, I heard Sam Sheedy shout 'Go on, Showboat!'

A big cheer went up and I saw how many people were there waiting for me to come out.

I stood in front of Buckingham Palace for ages, having pictures taken with people I didn't even know from all over the world. Then I had more pictures taken with family and friends who had travelled down, before we headed off to an after-party that we had organised.

It seemed to be a time of continual celebration as later that same year, we commemorated the 20-year anniversary of SBC opening on Burton Street. We decided to have a black-tie event at the Royal Victoria hotel, another great night with lots of boxing people invited. The former light-heavyweight world champion, John Conteh appeared as guest speaker and all the kids from the gym looked terrific in their tuxedos.

When all the summer parties were over, Dave Coldwell rang me again, unexpectedly. He wanted to know if I fancied putting Serge in a rematch with Jerome Wilson on his next show at Ice Sheffield. Just as before, I couldn't understand why he would want to do this. The last fight had been so tough for both boxers, especially Wilson. I thought Coldwell should have brought his fighter back with an easier bout than a rematch with Serge. Something to rebuild his confidence and get his career moving in the right direction again.

Just as I had the previous time, I asked him what his motivations were. He told me that he had signed a deal with the country's biggest promoter, Eddie Hearn, for something called 'Matchroom Fight Pass' which would be televised. The show was set to be the first one involved in this new deal, and he knew that a Wilson v Ambomo rematch would make great TV.

I was pretty repulsed by what I was hearing. It sounded to me like he was willing to sacrifice his own fighter to make this new TV venture successful. From our side, the arrangement was great business, mainly because Serge was such a difficult guy to match. He didn't sell tickets as he had no friends or family in England, but he was so ferocious that most promoters did not want to use him as an opponent for their boxers. The TV deal made for a higher purse, and I felt confident, as I had the first time, that Serge would win.

The rematch brought a great deal of local hype, becoming one of those events that everyone in Sheffield seemed to be talking about. If I went to buy a coffee or a sandwich somewhere, or stopped for petrol at a garage, I was asked how the preparations were going and whether I was confident. I always said I was, although Serge had some problems making weight for this one. With a week to go he was still way over where he needed to be, but somehow crashed it off and hit welterweight on the scales at his first attempt.

On the night, inside a very steamy, raucous arena, the fight was similar to the first. The longer it went on, the more you got the sense that Wilson was struggling to keep up. Serge put Wilson down in the second and kept coming. It was all Wilson could do to fend him off. In the fifth, Serge got through with a number of heavy shots. After the bell rang, before we sent Serge out for the sixth, I told Matt in our corner that I thought whoever was in charge in the Wilson camp should think about pulling him out. He looked exhausted, and you don't want to be in a ring with someone like Serge Ambomo when you've run out of gas.

I told Serge to just keep doing the same thing he'd been doing throughout the fight, which was obvious advice, because that was all Serge ever did. The sixth rapidly turned into another intense session, during which Serge pursued and pursued Wilson until he caught him with a big left hook that had him wobbling. He then followed up with a massive right, which sent Wilson toppling towards the canvas. Serge, being Serge, continued swinging and caught Wilson with a couple more shots as he fell. The momentum of these final punches caused Serge to lose his balance and he fell to the canvas on top of Jerome.

Immediately, from the way he had gone down, I knew Wilson was in a bad way. The referee started counting and without thinking I leapt into the ring to help Wilson's recovery.

Then everything turned nasty.

As Jerome lay on his back and I made my way towards the fighters, Serge bent over and kissed Wilson on his head, as if kissing him goodnight. This was way over the top, although difficult to see, as Wilson was laid out on the canvas and completely unconscious.

Serge jumped up, and I quickly turned Wilson on to his side then took out his gumshield while the paramedics got into the ring. The referee finally twigged and stopped counting. As soon as the medical team arrived, I stood and looked around, to see Serge standing by the ropes making the throat-cutting gesture at the crowd again, as he had against Adam Salman in London.

The whole venue just erupted in anger. This was a hotly anticipated local grudge match. One of the fighters was out cold and emotions were running high. People were screaming all kinds of awful, racist abuse at Serge, while Jerome's family at ringside were in pieces.

Jerome was stretchered out of the ring, to be taken to hospital. It was a very confused and volatile atmosphere, but we managed to make our way back to the changing rooms. Once we had battled our way through the crowd, someone knocked on the door and said Wilson was being treated and was in a bad way. My guts froze inside me, and I kept thinking, '*Not this again. Please, not this.*'

I told Serge to go home and said I would let him know if I heard anything. I then went back into the arena and asked random officials what they had heard. Information was sparse. All we knew was that Jerome Wilson's life was in the balance.

30

WITH A heavy heart, I started to drive home. All I could think about was Michael Watson, then young Bradley Stone, after Richie Wenton stopped him. I felt it was history repeating itself. Without even fully realising I had done it, I adjusted my route and found myself pulling up at the Royal Hallamshire Hospital. I knew I couldn't do anything to help, but for some reason I just felt compelled to go.

As I parked and made my way inside, I wondered how I would be received by Jerome's family. After all, I was the trainer of the boxer who had just put their kid in intensive care. I got in the lift and found myself shaking uncontrollably.

When the lift doors opened, I walked into a waiting area to see Dave Coldwell and the chairman of the Central Area BBBoC with Jerome's dad. No one knew what to say to each other. Words are always inadequate at times like that. The strangeness of the atmosphere started to make me feel upset, but I made an effort to hold it in for the sake of Jerome's father.

After what felt like an eternity of waiting, a doctor appeared and told everyone that an emergency operation was needed. Jerome was unconscious and he said he would come back to let everyone know if there had been any change in a few hours.

We all sat there like figures in a bad dream, making chit-chat. The whole thing was a haze for me. I didn't even know why I was there and being around Coldwell began to bug me. By 3.45am, I drew the conclusion that we could be waiting a long time for news and there was no point staying up all night, so I said goodbye to Jerome's dad and left.

Over the next few days, the events around the fight built into quite a furore, both inside and outside Sheffield. It made national news. All the media outlets were discussing it. Wilson had suffered a subdural haematoma, a type of brain bleed, had an operation to remove part of his skull and was in a coma. No one knew if he would live or die.

There was uproar about what Serge had done, which as his trainer and manager, reflected on me. Kissing Jerome on the head and making the throat-cutting gesture would have been bad enough if Wilson had got up and been fine 20 seconds later. Those kinds of actions would have been guaranteed to provoke a very strong reaction from the public, but bearing in mind Jerome's condition, it looked ghoulish in retrospect. No one wants that in boxing. Serge had crossed a line.

I spoke to Serge about what happened. He had the attitude of a Roman gladiator. He was impassive.

'It was me or him,' he said with a shrug.

I found it callous and it was difficult for me to accept. Throughout the many years I had been involved in boxing I had never been able to brush off death or serious injury. We all know it's possible, but when it happens you feel terrible and want to reach out to those affected. 'There but for the grace of God, go I,' as the old saying goes. I just hoped beyond anything that Wilson survived and was able to get some sort of life back.

I told Serge to at least say he was sorry, but he didn't understand. I didn't want him to apologise for knocking Wilson out, but for his macabre showmanship afterwards. I felt he should apologise not only to Jerome, but publicly. He needed to explain that it had all been a heat-of-the-moment thing after a fierce battle and that he regretted his actions. Otherwise, it could all have serious repercussions for his career. I suggested that he send a get-well-soon message to the hospital, and that he should say these things even if he really didn't mean them. But Serge was having none of it.

As often happens when some sort of tragedy occurs, there was bitterness on all sides. Serge was angry that people were criticising him even though he won. He was justifiably upset by the racial abuse he received and apparently, which was news to me, there had been a lot of bad blood between the two camps, with vicious messages exchanged on social media, both before and after the fight.

I did think that it might be a cultural thing, that as a Cameroonian, Serge's attitudes to life and death were different to someone from the UK. This was definitely possible, but even with that thought in mind, I found myself unable to move past it. I wasn't able to square Serge's outlook with my own feelings. At the time, Wilson could still have died. Even if he emerged from the coma, no one knew what sort of state he would be in. His family, including a girlfriend and their young children were frantic with worry. You can't treat people like that.

I had pre-existing doubts about Serge anyway, back from the fight with Adam Salman at York Hall, but his heartlessness in this situation was the final straw. Our relationship ended and I never worked with him again. He was suspended by the BBBoC for his actions that night and asked for his contract back shortly afterwards.

For the next few days, I thought about Jerome Wilson day and night, and went through a period of sleeplessness. I stayed updated on his situation by communicating with his brother and was relieved to be told that, after a week and a half, he began to emerge from the coma.

I waited a few weeks, then went to visit him in hospital. By the time I arrived he was talking and smiling again and seemed in good spirits. He head was a strange shape, owing to the piece of skull that had been removed. You couldn't help but look at it.

A strange stew of emotions stirred inside me as a result of that visit. I went to my gym and got on with the day-to-day stuff that I always did, but with a kind of bleakness inside. It's hard to live the boxing life when you've seen the worst that it can do.

How could I, in good conscience, train a six or seven-year-old kid to box, then chat to his mum about how he's doing, when I knew that the end result, at some point in the future, could be what happened to Wilson, Watson or even worse, Stone? How do I square that within myself? Again, I was forced to acknowledge that although boxing had given me so much and had raised my life out of the ordinary, it could take so much too.

It made me think of the yin yang symbol, used in Eastern philosophy and martial arts. The light in the darkness and the darkness in the light. At that time, that summarised how I felt about boxing and also about myself. It's not easy, when you devote your life to something, then find yourself questioning it, but after the Wilson–Ambomo rematch, and at 54 years old, that's where I was at.

Despite that, I got on with things as best I could and after a while, I suppose everything began to feel more normal again. Time has that effect.

By the summer of 2016, several SBC fighters, in particular Sam Sheedy and Scott Westgarth, were making great progress, while my flyweight Tommy Frank had turned over and was preparing for his debut.

We all had to cope with the devastating news of Muhammad Ali's death in June, which was a big blow to me. I don't mind admitting I cried when I heard the news, then went straight to a travel agent and told them I wanted to book a flight to Louisville, Kentucky, Ali's hometown. I told no one I was going, packed a few things and drove to Manchester Airport.

When I arrived, Louisville was full of banners hanging from streetlights bearing Ali's picture. The city was packed with people like me who had made their way to Louisville to pay their respects and the following morning I woke up early to make my way to the Muhammad Ali Museum.

As so often seemed to happen to me, I coincidentally met a guy outside the museum who was an Englishman living in Louisville. He told me about a private ceremony that had taken place to inter Ali's body at Cave Hill Cemetery and asked if I would like to go. It was a lovely touch of kindness from a total stranger, which meant I got to see Ali's final resting place.

The grave was surprisingly low-key. No big monument, no headstone. We got out of the car and stood there for a while. The area was full of flowers and flags from all over the world, which were a reminder of the impact this man had. He wasn't just an American hero, but a global one.

I felt a sense of peace afterwards, spent a few more days there, visited Ali's childhood home and the bridge where he allegedly threw his gold medal into the river. That satisfied my need to make a pilgrimage and I was able to return home, feeling that I had paid my respects.

Back in England, Sam Sheedy was training for an eliminator for the British and Commonwealth title, on the same show as Tommy Frank's debut.

Sam boxed a kid called Andrew Robinson over ten rounds, showed plenty of courage, gritted his teeth and managed to win on points despite carrying a back injury into the bout. That win meant he was now in place to challenge for major domestic honours. Tommy outpointed a tough Russian journeyman too, making it a good night for our gym.

A while after that, a British and Commonwealth title fight was arranged between Chris Eubank Jr and Tommy Langford for October in Cardiff, but then Eubank decided to relinquish the British title and withdraw from the fight. The show was a Queensberry Promotions event, and I got a call from someone in Frank Warren's office, who now needed a new opponent for their headline fight.

They asked if I would be interested in putting Sam Sheedy in for the vacant British title against Langford and

I jumped at the chance. Sam was 28 by this time and had paid his dues.

In the early autumn, I got one of those phone calls that you often get in this game. The fight with Sheedy and Langford was to be postponed until November, which was something of a pain in the arse for us, as we had been geared up for the original date and it meant a lot of readjusting.

By the time the fight eventually rolled around, Sam's head seemed to be in a pretty good place. We had some fun at the weigh-in with Sam's new gimmick of wearing a sombrero to his public appearances. One of the media asked why he was wearing it and he replied that he was a third-generation Mexican, which some people actually seemed to believe. He weighed in bang on the middleweight limit.

In the end, the fight turned into one of those nip and tuck boxing matches that could go either way. Sam had been the aggressor throughout and taken the fight to Langford at times, but Langford had been busy behind the jab. Ultimately, Sam lost a knife-edge split decision, which was tough to swallow. At least he showed he belonged at that level, and I felt sure that he would pick up another title sooner or later.

31

REGARDLESS OF whatever else happened in my boxing career, the rift that had grown between myself and Brendan never stopped bothering me. Over the years there had been quite a few occasions when I had found myself in the same room as him and I just wanted to make things right. We were both ageing. He was 76 by this time and beginning to look frail, whereas I was in my mid-fifties. Why did we need to carry on this silly dispute?

When someone gets into their seventies, you never really know how long they have left. One thing I knew for sure was that I did not want Brendan to die without us having a chance to make up. To him, I might have been just another boxer, but he had been too important to me for too long to allow things to end like that.

At the time there was a light-heavyweight training at the Ingle gym called Amer Khan (not to be confused with Amir Khan, the former light-welterweight world champion). I saw him at an event, where he said he knew about the history between Brendan and I and that he wanted to help. He told me he would speak to Brendan and set up a meeting. I didn't think too much of it.

Khan surprised me by phoning me a few days later. He said he had set up a meeting with Brendan at St Thomas', which made me a little uneasy. I would have preferred neutral ground. The gym would likely be full of his boxers and there was the chance of a nasty atmosphere.

I asked if Brendan had been happy to meet with me and he replied that he had, but that his wife, Alma, was not too enthused. When I arrived at the agreed time, it was an extremely strange feeling. I had not returned to St Thomas' since leaving in 1993, but the place had been a massive part of my life for 18 years.

As I walked in, my mind was going a hundred miles an hour, remembering so many scenes I had witnessed in that space. Amer came to meet me in the doorway and as I shook his hand, I saw Brendan leaning on the wall halfway down the gym, as he so often used to do.

My heart raced as I looked around. The gym was full and I recognised some of the fighters, but not all of them.

Alma walked towards me at that point. I thought she was coming to greet me, so I smiled.

'Hello, Alma,' I said.

She completely blanked me and walked past, which upset me a little. Amer saw this happen, put his arm round me and said, 'Come on.'

He began to lead me toward Brendan, who had not moved an inch since I first came in. It was like he was frozen, just watching. Brendan's son Dominic was leading the session.

'Stop training, lads!' Dominic shouted. 'Come and gather round here.'

I could see the young kids looking at me and wondering what was going on.

'There's been lots of people pass through this gym over the years,' Dom said. 'And some have gone on to bigger and better things but there's only two boxing people in Sheffield been awarded MBEs from the Queen and they are my dad and Glyn Rhodes. Today we have a very special guest who has come to speak to my dad.'

He gestured at me, and everyone clapped. Brendan and I had both brought our MBE medals and held them for some pictures.

'This fella used to be a horrible bastard!' Brendan quipped.

I couldn't help but laugh. 'You're not wrong there, Brendan.'

'He should have been a world champion, but he wouldn't listen.'

'Look, everyone,' I said. 'The truth is that I owe Brendan so much. Most of what I have got and achieved is down to him. He changed my life and I'll always be grateful.'

Everyone clapped again, and then drifted off back to training. I had brought a black-and-white picture with me. It was of Brendan working my corner in an amateur fight when I was 16 years old. I asked him if he would sign it and he took a long look at the picture before asking if I wanted him to sign his normal signature. He seemed quite shaky and unsure of himself, and I didn't know what he meant by that. It was sad to see him looking so old, but I recognised that I must have aged in his eyes, too.

We talked for a while, and I asked him if he remembered the days of secret training. On one of them we had all lifted the girders through the walls of the gym to hang the bags. I also pointed out that there was one picture hanging on the wall of the gym that I had made years before, which was still hanging in the same place. We had a lovely chat and just as I said goodbye, he leaned in towards me.

'Glen,' he said, with a grin. 'Glen, I've got yous a fight.' My eyes welled up.

'Thanks, Brendan,' I said and left.

As I walked out, I was stopped by a young fighter called Adam Etches who told me he admired what I had said to all the boxers and shook my hand. I thanked him before I went.

I left feeling so pleased I made that journey down to St Thomas'. It felt like all the nonsense of the previous 20-odd years had been put to bed, which was such a relief. No one needs all that negative energy.

By the middle of 2017, Sam Sheedy had been lined up for a Commonwealth title shot. His showing against Langford had been strong enough to keep him in contention and he was set to face a Nigerian called Rasheed Abolaji. We knew that these guys from West Africa either come over here just for a pay day, or they are tough, strong, spirited fighters. We prepared for the latter. It was a good job we did.

Sam prepared well for this one and the mood in the camp was positive. When we arrived at the arena, it was strange to see Clinton Woods in the same dressing room. Since losing to Tavoris Cloud in Florida a few years back, he had become a trainer and his light-heavyweight prospect Joss Paul was fighting on the same bill. This is what I mean about British boxing being a small world. There are only around a thousand active fighters in the country. Each of them has a handful of people in tow, a manager, a promoter, a trainer etc, so it means professional boxing as a sport is only comprised of a few thousand people. Set within an overall population of 68 million, it's clear how compact it is, and why we all know each other so well.

When the time came to get ready, Sam, as usual, had a couple of problems. He was always a fighter that needed certain reassurances before getting in the ring. I tended to think it was more in his head than anything, but he had brought a girl called Lisa to massage his back. We all waited around while he had his back massage. When it was finished, Sam jumped up like nothing was wrong, and Matt and I exchanged a smirk. I guess if it helped him to settle, then it was okay.

Once we got in there, Abolaji looked a real specimen. He had muscles on his ears. I told Sam to keep out of the way for the first round, so we could see how the opponent shaped up. That went okay, so after the first, I told Sam to start sitting down on his shots, to try to deter his opponent from walking forward so much.

The second round was much like the first, though, and I was not pleased. Once Sam came back, I gave him a bollocking in the corner. Sam was better than the Nigerian, but I didn't want him to miss out on the chance for a major title by fighting the wrong fight. As I climbed out of the ring, Matt had a word in my ear.

'Try not to shout at Sam,' he said. 'It just upsets him.'

This had been something that had come up before, but sometimes in the heat of battle, with limited time, it was the only way to get your point across.

As the fight progressed, I couldn't help shouting at Sam. There were times I would ask him to do something, and he would say, 'Yes, Glyn', then go out and do the complete opposite.

By the mid-point of the fight, he started arguing back and I sensed a bit of panic in his voice. In the end it was tight. Sam got hurt a couple of times and had to slip and slide to get through it, but just about squeezed home and got the decision.

As the announcer called his name, and the crowd roared, we all jumped in the air. In many ways it was one of my most special moments. For me to take this kid from an 11-year-old all the way to a major title was something very important to me, personally.

Despite that, the following Monday felt like a real gut punch, when I picked up the local newspaper and the main headline on the sports page declared that Sam Sheedy might sack his training team.

I read the article and it seemed Sam had given an interview in which he said how upset he was with me shouting at him in the corner, that I had stopped him concentrating. He claimed that's why he boxed as shakily as he did.

My phone rang constantly throughout the morning, so I called Sam to find out what was going on. He stuck to his guns and insisted I shouldn't have shouted at him, so we agreed to disagree and put it behind us. He apologised and said he didn't really want to fire me.

Still, the whole thing provided another reality check. As a boxing trainer you can do ten things right and no one says anything, but when there are issues, you immediately get the blame.

More than that, you can work with a fighter for 18 years, man and boy, and still get slagged off publicly by them. I felt a headache coming on.

Never mind. At least I had a Commonwealth champion.

32

SAM'S NEXT fight was against Liam Cameron in defence of his Commonwealth title. Both kids were from Sheffield, so it was hotly anticipated and promoted as a great local derby. In truth, I wasn't too happy about the fight, purely because it was on a Dennis Hobson show, and Liam was managed by Dennis.

Sam's mental state, which was often a bit all over the place didn't seem right at all, and he pulled out of the fight. It was rescheduled for 13 October 2017.

In the weeks that followed I began to get a little worried about him. He started talking about retiring and said that the fight didn't motivate him. I told him there would be bigger things on the horizon once he beat Liam Cameron and said he should win easily. I only told Sam this to try to motivate him into getting back in the gym, but it didn't work.

He would turn up when everyone else was finishing, or sometimes before they all started. He had loads of problems outside the ring and too many demons in his head. It was clear he wasn't right. As his trainer and friend, I stuck by him and tried my best to get him in the right frame of mind. I told him that without boxing he didn't have anything and if he stopped, he would lose all his sponsorship. How would he get by? He just nodded and said, 'Yes, you're right,' but still didn't come to the gym to train as much as he should have.

The closer we came to fight night, the harder and harder I found it to work with Sam. He was talking bollocks all the time. I found out that AJ, Dennis Hobson's nephew had been giving Sheedy money, which seemed a very messy situation, bearing in mind that he was fighting Hobson's fighter.

The weeks up to the show were hard work, as it became steadily more obvious that Sheedy's head was all over the place. I began to wonder what the hell I was doing and whether the whole thing was worth it.

It got to the point that I just couldn't wait to get the fight out of the way, so I didn't have to see Sam for a while. I know this sounds awful as we had worked together since he was 11, but every day was the same old shit. Sam would talk about jacking it all in and I had to try to talk him round. It was mentally exhausting.

Before the weigh-in, I wanted Sam to come to the gym to check his weight on the scales first, but Sam turned up late with his girlfriend then told her to follow us in her car. He sat in the passenger seat next to me and would not shut up. I really felt something wasn't right with him.

Despite all that, he weighed in well. The fighters were respectful to each other and the pre-fight routine all seemed relatively normal.

Once they got in there, it was really noticeable how much bigger Liam looked than Sam and it turned into a truly depressing evening. Sam's performance was flat and lacking in energy. Cameron just walked forward without any real flair or imagination. It was almost as if Sam was letting him win.

In the corner I tried reasoning and pleading with him. When those didn't work, I shouted again but most of the time Sam just slumped on his stool as if he was asleep. At one point I went absolutely ballistic and asked if he wanted to stay champion.

'Yeah!' he shouted. It was pretty much the only time I got a reaction out of him and briefly afterwards, he fought better too. But it didn't last long.

Sam behaved as if his head was on another planet. He went down three times in the fourth round and twice in the seventh. I couldn't believe he was allowing himself to get knocked around like that. Sam should have boxed his ears off.

In the eighth, everything turned surreal. Sam just stood in front of Cameron, inviting him to punch him, which, naturally, is what Liam did. Sam basically stopped defending himself and took some hefty shots before the referee rightly stopped the fight. I dragged him back to the corner. He was groggy and rubber-lipped. Once he came around I asked what the hell he had been playing at.

'I've had enough,' Sam said. 'I just wanted him to knock me out.'

I honestly did not know what to say to that.

Back in the changing room, the doctor came in to have a look at Sam and seemed a little panicked. Security got everyone out, which angered Sam's girlfriend as she was shepherded outside, but meant that the doctors could give Sam a thorough check.

They went through their tests, then one doctor turned to the other and whispered, 'Bleed on the brain.'

I felt like I was underwater. Everything went blurry and sickness rose in my guts. Boxing was doing too much of this to me, and too often. The doctors said that Sam needed immediate hospital attention, so Matt and I began to pack away frantically.

Sam was stretchered to the ambulance, and I was told I could travel with him. As we raced through the streets with the sirens blaring, my thoughts went back to the times I had been in similar situations.

The hospital was a typical hospital scene on a Saturday night. Lots of drunkards and people who had had silly accidents. They wheeled Sam into a room with two beds. The other had a guy on it laying prone, with policemen standing either side of him. My head was swimming with the insanity of it and all I could think of was how irritated I had been with Sam before the night. Right then, I would have given one of my kidneys just to know he would be okay.

After a while, Sam started talking. Nothing very coherent at first, but I took that to be a positive sign. Various tests and examinations were conducted over the course of the next few hours, until the doctors said they didn't think there was any serious damage, although they wanted to keep him there overnight as a precaution.

I made my way home in a state of extreme exhaustion, but still found it hard to sleep. At 10am the next day I was due in the gym. I forced myself to drive there wearily, dreading what was coming. I knew what everyone would be talking about. Sam's girlfriend came in to speak to me and told me Sam's career was over. She said he couldn't cope with the pressure. I had to agree with her.

So that was it. After what had been an up-and-down, seventeen-year ride, Sam 'Speedy' Sheedy was gone too. He stayed around the gym, as Matt Mowatt had, wanting to become a coach, but my training focus shifted to other lads like Tommy Frank and Scott Westgarth. Tommy was 5-0 by then and heading towards an area title fight, while Scott had recovered superbly after his debut setback, had won five of eight, with one draw, and was on the cusp of minor title contention himself.

This focus was sharpened when Carl Wild retired too. He boxed his last fight just before Christmas 2017, against

Joss Paul for the Central Area cruiserweight title. Carl gave a good account of himself, thankfully. He had looked pretty slow in sparring beforehand, and I had been worried, but he hung in there throughout the ten rounds and showed his spirit. Afterwards, I found Carl crying backstage. He had known it was going to be his last contest, but it's still a tough thing to accept. I ended up crying with him for about ten minutes.

Anyone looking would have wondered what was going on. Two tough ex-boxers sobbing their hearts out all over each other, but fighters can be an emotional bunch.

As I reflected at the end of the year, one thing I had to admit was that the constant trauma boxing was inflicting on me was beginning to take its toll. I still had a deep love for the sport and knew I could never separate myself from it. Without boxing, I would be nothing, but my sleeplessness got worse and became habitual. Some days I felt like I wasn't fully there. I also noticed that I often drifted off, thinking of some of the things I had seen, as if my mind was processing them in some way. Someone could even be talking to me, and I would be lost in visions of Jerome Wilson with a chunk of skull missing, Sam Sheedy in the ambulance, Bradley Stone in his corner, or Michael Watson on the stretcher. It wasn't something I was able to switch off from.

Of course, I had no idea at the time, but these sorts of feelings were about to be multiplied by a few hundred per cent.

33

2018 BEGAN badly and then tailed off from there. Just after New Year, my friend and former British title challenger Chris Walker died. He was only in his early sixties. Then an old mate of mine from Hull, Steve Pollard, a former area champion, was diagnosed with motor neurone disease. To cap it off, shortly after hearing about those two, I received a phone call to say that Herol Graham had been sectioned.

I went down to see him in London, where he was being kept in a mental hospital. It was a horrible experience. I didn't think Bomber should have been in there but told myself that the doctors knew best. He seemed bleary-eyed and a bit incoherent. I guess they were keeping him on some sort of medication. He was pleased to see me, at least. It was so strange to see him there like that because I still thought of Herol as a lithe, flashy teenager with the world at his feet, the kid who no one could hit. Life had managed to get to him in the end, it seemed.

Dwelling on these depressing things was not an option though, as on 24 February I had Scott Westgarth fighting Dec

Spelman, from Scunthorpe, in an eliminator for the English title, to be staged in Doncaster. It was a big one for SBC, bearing in mind the fighters who had recently retired, and it would be a great achievement for Scott if he won, considering his late start and how his career had begun.

Training went superbly as it always did with Scott. He was a great pro who lived the life, and always looked after himself between fights.

We knew it was going to be a tough contest as Dec Spelman had destroyed Carl Wild in the second round a couple of years previously. Our expectation was that he would come out aggressively, so our plan was to weather the storm of the first three rounds, then give him a boxing lesson. Scott had become quite an accomplished jab-and-move type fighter by this time.

Both fighters had very vocal crowds in attendance, which surprised me, bearing in mind Spelman's fans had come all the way from Lincolnshire. It made for an electric atmosphere.

Just as we had expected, Dec came out all guns blazing at the first bell. Scott managed to fend him off and by the middle of the third, Spelman started to slow down. Scott immediately took control, doubling up on the jab and giving Dec a boxing lesson. Towards the end of the round, Scott threw a one-two and put Spelman down. Beautiful.

I jumped up, feeling that it was the beginning of the end. When you've been totally outboxed, then find yourself on your backside, it's a horrible feeling. Spelman climbed off the floor and continued ploughing forward, but it really looked like Scotty had his number.

In round nine, Dec caught Scott with a good shot, which wobbled him. Both kids were very tired by this point, and Spelman was unable to take advantage.

We sent Scott out for the last round feeling that he had the fight won. I told him to keep sticking the jab out and he would have a title fight to look forward to. Spelman knew the fight was slipping away, so gave it everything and managed to catch Scott again. They got tangled up and both fighters ended up on the canvas, with Scotty almost falling out of the ring. I ran to the side of the ring, pushed him back in and, as he stood up, the bell rang to end the fight.

We all jumped in the ring and celebrated. I looked over to the former world cruiserweight champion Glenn McCrory who was commentating for TV and he gave me a nod to say he had it for us. Scott leaned over the ropes in exhaustion, but I told him to stand up and raise his hands because he needed to look like a winner.

The emcee announced the decision and sure enough, Scott had won. It was a great moment for him and well deserved. But from that point on, everything changed.

I went to wipe Scott's face with a towel and, as I did so, he staggered backwards. I wasn't too concerned, because he had just done ten hard-fought rounds and I put it down to tired legs. Then the TV people asked to interview Scott at ringside. There were no steps to get out of the ring, so I told them we would come down the stairs in our corner and walk around to do the interview.

I asked the house second to hold Scott as he climbed out of the ring, as he was a little shaky, but this is quite normal for a fighter who has just been the distance.

Scott did the interview and spoke well, but towards the end he sat down on the ring apron and rubbed his head. I thought he was just exhausted, but as we walked back to the changing rooms, I noticed he was unstable on his legs.

A few fears began floating in the back of my mind, but I tried to keep them under control. There's a fine line between caution and paranoia. Once we got back to our changing room, Scott complained about a pain in his neck and said that he thought he had pulled a muscle when he fell out of the ring. He laid on the floor in the changing room. I put a towel over his eyes as he lay blinking in the lights.

Scott asked for a drink of Lucozade, sat up and guzzled it. As soon as the drink went down, he vomited. I could smell it on the floor, mixed with bile. It was disgusting.

The doctor arrived, had a look at Scott and said he wanted him to go to the hospital, to get checked out. The paramedics came with a stretcher, but Scott said, 'I'm not getting on that.

I'll walk to the ambulance.' I was encouraged by that and thought it meant he was probably okay.

The doctors insisted, so eventually Scott caved in and got on the stretcher. They asked who would be riding in the ambulance with him and I felt it was my duty as his manager and trainer, so I said I would do it. I asked Carl Wild to grab all my gear and Scott's clothes, then security led the way out of the venue. All the while a little voice in the back of my head kept saying how it couldn't believe this was happening again. I just couldn't seem to escape this side of the game.

People stood around crying as we climbed into the ambulance. Everything was a blur. The paramedic shut the doors and motioned for me to sit on a chair beside the gurney. As the ambulance started moving, the doctor spoke to Scott, just chatting. Scotty said he felt sick. The doctor opened a small cupboard, pulled out a sick bag and passed it to him.

Scott tried to sit up but was strapped to the gurney. He was sick in the bag, then laid back down. He retched again, turned to his side, spewed in the bag, then fell backwards on to the gurney.

'Stay with me, Scott!' the doctor shouted. 'Stay with me, stay with me!'

The ambulance was bouncing all over the road, as the doctor rummaged in the cupboards over the gurney, pulling items out, as if he was preparing something.

I started shouting at Scott too, although I had no idea what was going on. A feeling of panic overcame me. 'Come on Scotty, stay awake!'

He seemed to be drifting out of consciousness and I knew he was supposed to be going on holiday with his girlfriend to a log cabin somewhere, so I thought I could use that.

'Natalie can't wait for your holiday, Scotty. She told me all about the resort!'

His eyes began to close.

At that point, the doctor took out a large pair of scissors and cut the sleeve of Scott's puffa jacket straight up the arm. He needed access to an artery, and that was the quickest way to do it. A flurry of feathers emerged from the incision in the material and floated about in the air.

I was still holding Scott's hand while the doctor was inserting a needle into Scotty's arm and at the same time, I was trying to blow all the feathers away, so they didn't obstruct what he was doing. They kept boomeranging back at me and sticking to my nose. The whole scene was so bizarre. It felt like a nightmare. I know people always say that in these situations, but it really did.

The doctor shouted to the driver to stop the ambulance, as he couldn't get the needle in the right place. By this point the ambulance was flying down roads and hurtling around corners. Unbelievably, the whole scene was all still about to get worse.

Suddenly, Scott's back arched, his head bent behind him, and his chin went in the air. At the same time, his eyes rolled up into his head, like something from a horror film.

I found myself transfixed, unable to look away from his face. Scott's eyes were open, but he had no pupils or irises, just white, which frightened me on some really deep, instinctive level. It was a fear I could feel from my legs all the way up my body.

'Stay with me!' the doctor screamed again. There was emotion in his voice. All the while, the feathers fluttered around.

It seemed to take forever, as I sat there, still holding Scott's arm, his body convulsing intermittently. The rest of the world stopped existing. It was just the three of us in that tiny, claustrophobic space until at last, the ambulance slowed as it went over the speed bumps into the hospital. The back doors flew open, and the feathers blew around like crazy as the stretcher was pulled off the ambulance.

They ran inside, but no one said anything to me, so I just followed them straight through the doors, into a treatment room where lots of medics rushed around, shouting at each other. Amid the chaos, I realised I had one of Scott's trainers in my hand. I'm not sure why, but this provided a little jolt back to reality. It was like I woke up and thought, *'Fuck, I'm stood here like a lamppost, with all this madness whirling around me, holding a shoe.'*

They lifted Scott off the gurney, put him on a hospital bed and the doctors convened an emergency meeting. The doctor from the ambulance told everyone else what had happened, then the whole lot of them leapt into action. It was like I was having an out-of-body experience. I was in the room, but no one knew I was there. I felt invisible.

They started doing things to Scott, at which point my presence was noticed and a nurse came over and told me to go with her. My heart was pounding, and I felt like I could very easily collapse myself. I was told to sit in the family room.

After a short while, Carl Wild arrived, followed by Scott's girlfriend and his dad. No one said anything.

I walked out after a few minutes as I didn't feel able to sit with Natalie (Scott's girlfriend). I had no idea what to say to her and was still badly shaken myself. When I came back, she was hysterical because the paramedic had told her that Scott might have a bleed on the brain.

I told her to try to be calm, because until they had given Scott a scan no one could know for sure. Internally, I didn't believe my own soothing words. I knew Scott was in grave danger and had never witnessed anything as horrible as what happened in that ambulance.

We were told that Scott needed to be moved to the Hallamshire Hospital in Sheffield for an operation. Carl Wild gave me a lift there and on the way my phone rang and beeped constantly. We arrived just before midnight, ran through the main doors, went up in the lift and were shown to another family room. I didn't say anything, but it was the same one I had sat in when Jerome Wilson was injured several years before. I bowed my head. I didn't like this room at all. I certainly did not want to be in it again.

No one knew what to say or do. We drank tea from the vending machine and paced up and down. At one in the morning, we were told Scott had arrived from Doncaster. A doctor told us what he would be doing. He confirmed that Scott had a bleed and started talking about putting something into Scott's head. He said he had done three of these operations before, which made us all feel a bit better, as if all this was somehow more normal. He also told us about percentages and that while carrying out the operation, there was a chance Scott could have a stroke or a heart attack, but we wouldn't know any of this until it was over. Before leaving, he said that someone would come back later to tell us how the operation had gone.

Just as before, we drank tea and mooched about. The hours dragged on through to 5am, until the doctor returned and asked to speak to the family in another room. That jolted me. A sense of dread made my throat dry and hung heavily in my chest.

Scott's family went with the doctor while the rest of us sat there and waited. We soon understood. The scream that I heard come through that wall will live with me for the rest of my life.

It was followed by howling and crying. There were shouts of 'No, please no!'

All of us, waiting helplessly, knew what that meant.

34

I WANTED to run away, but where could I run to? Everyone was crying and asking, 'Why, why, why?' Of course, no one knew why.

I walked up and down the hospital. Only a few hours before I had been sitting in the changing room with Scott, getting ready. Everything had been good. This couldn't possibly be happening. He was fit and well prepared. He even won the fight, for God's sake! I was there with him when the ref raised his hand, listening to the cheering crowd.

Stuff like this doesn't happen to winners. All the boxing tragedies I had known before were the result of the fighter being knocked out. I just couldn't make sense of it.

I tried to phone my girlfriend a couple of times. We had been seeing each other for a little while by this time and I thought her voice would make me feel better, but she had switched her phone off.

Her job as a physiotherapist in the NHS often meant early starts, so I knew she was in bed. Nonetheless it bothered me.

She was the one person I wanted to speak to, and I couldn't get hold of her.

The doctor told us they would clean Scott up and bring him back up to the ward, so we could all say goodbye to him. I thought, 'What the fuck are you talking about? Say goodbye to him? What's that supposed to mean? Say goodbye to him. It's like he's going abroad or something.'

As the doctor walked away, those words kept repeating in my head.

You can say goodbye to him.

I wanted to scream at him. 'How can you say that? There must be something the hospital can do. How can he be dead? Someone needs to sort this …'

I felt dizzy and sat on the floor, but just couldn't take in what was going on.

You can say goodbye to him.

Some bloke tried to hug me. I didn't have a clue who he was and pushed him away. I saw Carl Wild crying, leaning on the wall, so I walked over to him. We hugged each other and it was like neither of us wanted to let go.

After a while, Scott's dad, John Westgarth came over to us.

'You can go and see him now,' he said. At that moment, I wasn't sure I wanted to see Scotty. I had never seen a dead person before in my life, let alone someone I had spent so much time with, but John seemed to be the calmest person in the hospital that night. He put his arms around me and said, 'You have to promise me.'

'Promise what?' I asked.

'You have to promise me you will keep going to that gym.'

I hadn't even thought about the gym, but John said it again. 'Promise me.'

'Okay, John. I will.'

So, we followed John to the room where Scotty lay. I found myself struggling to walk in through the door, but John was behind me and put his hand on my shoulder. A nurse stood by the body, and reluctantly my eyes were drawn to Scott's face.

He looked peaceful, like he was asleep, with a big bandage on his head. Immediately, I started crying uncontrollably, an instinctive reaction over which I had no control. It just poured out of me.

I walked over to the bed, reached out, put my hand on his shoulder, then bent down and kissed him on his cheek. I can't remember what I said, but I whispered something, then turned and walked out of that room.

I went downstairs with Carl Wild, both of us crying our eyes out and as we got to the main entrance and looked out at the car park, we saw one of Scott's friends who had just arrived, struggling with his little white dogs. It was so weird as it was the first time I had set foot outside the hospital building for hours and suddenly it was like the world did still exist, with this little scene playing out in front of me.

This guy was trying to get the dogs out of the car, but one was pulling him one way and one the other. Something about watching this bloke struggle with his dogs was so heartwarming and funny. In a moment I switched from crying to laughing.

'Look at that idiot!' I said to Carl, through my nose. Carl started laughing too, both of us still with tears rolling down our cheeks.

Once we had pulled ourselves together enough to leave, Carl gave me a lift back to the gym as I had left my car there earlier in the day. It was daylight again by then and both of us spluttered with tears intermittently on the drive back.

It was seven in the morning when I got in. I tried to go to bed, but when my head touched the pillow and I closed my eyes, I just saw Scott in that ambulance with his eyes rolling back in his head and all the feathers flying around.

After a short while, I gave up, got out of bed, looked out of my kitchen window and saw three men walking up my drive. I didn't have a clue who they were, so went out and said, 'Hello.'

Of course, they were reporters. One of them asked for an interview, which I was in no way ready for. I calmly asked them to get back down my drive.

I had recently bought a Volkswagen Camper van, like the one Brendan used to have, so made a snap decision to put my push bike on the bike rack and drive to Castleton, a lovely village, surrounded by beautiful countryside, about four miles from Sheffield. After I arrived, I turned my phone off, pulled into a campsite to park, then went for a long walk.

There was something soothing in the hills and the sky and wind. It was a grey day, and pretty cold, but that suited me fine. I knew I needed some time alone.

I walked for a couple of hours, then kidded myself I was feeling better. I knew there would be lots of people wanting news, so turned my phone on and instantly regretted it. I was bombarded with messages and missed calls and had a quick look through, but it was too much for me. I didn't reply to any of them.

Eventually, my girlfriend finished her shift, called, then came out to meet me. We had dinner in a little café in the middle of nowhere, then walked back to the campsite. She asked me to go back to her place with her, but I shook my head. I still wanted to be alone.

By the time I got to bed that night, I had been up for 36 hours or so and was physically destroyed. Still, every time I closed my eyes, I found myself back in that ambulance looking at Scott, trying to blow the feathers away. That set a pattern for the weeks that followed.

For a while before Scott Westgarth's death, I had struggled with insomnia, but after Scotty died it was much worse. Sleep became a rarity, and I just couldn't function right. My head was in a mess, and it seemed to deteriorate every day. There were times I just wanted to take my brain out and put it in a jar or something for a bit, to give myself a rest.

Everyone at the gym was talking about Scotty non-stop and I took it upon myself to say the right things and provide a strong presence, to help others through their grief. The problem was that I was losing the battle with my own. The gym became like a shrine. There were flowers left at the door. People brought in photos and memorabilia.

I didn't feel that we would all ever get over it if that carried on, so after a week or so, I had to tell people to stop bringing in mementoes of Scott. We all needed a rest from it, especially me. I got the feeling that people still obsessed about it but stopped talking about it in front of me. In a way, that's what I wanted. I really didn't want to talk about what I had seen in the ambulance, so it made sense for me to bury it.

In the midst of all this turmoil and anguish, Tommy Frank got offered an area title fight at Ice Sheffield on 27 April 2018. The venue held bad memories for me from the Ambomo v Wilson fight, but what can you do? It felt like everywhere I went there were painful memories by then.

It was just boxing again. Boxing being boxing, always in the background. Here it comes again. One kid dies, another gets an opportunity. You just can't escape from it, like some mad, never-ending loop.

I agreed to the fight, because it was right for Tommy's career, but had no idea how I was going to cope. There were a million things going round in my head. What, I thought – and as a trainer it's so challenging to think like this – what if something bad happened to Tommy, now? Young Tommy who came to me at 11 years old. What the fuck would I do then?

Tommy's weigh-in was held at the venue and as I found myself walking into the Ice arena where Serge Ambomo had nearly killed Jerome Wilson a few years earlier, I felt extremely uncomfortable, but put on a brave face. How would I feel walking to the ring with Tommy the following day? I had no idea. The darker side of boxing seemed to dominate. The yin yang had faded away. Where was the light? I couldn't see it.

Tommy made the weight at 8 stone 2, with no bother, as I knew he would, then we all left to get some dinner. After, I went home and got my bag ready, something I had been doing for many years. This time, it was different. As I packed the hand-wraps, scissors and other bits I would need, I kept bursting into tears.

On fight night, we met at the venue, and all walked in together. Tommy had got t-shirts for everyone to wear with Scott's name and picture on them, and I found them difficult to look at. In the changing room, I began preparing Tommy, then sneaked off to the toilet, cried, washed my face and walked back into the changing room, trying to act normally.

When the time came to get Tommy ready, I taped his hands up and he started shadow boxing. Then I took him on the pads, to get him warm. All routine stuff. Again, I had to stop and pretend I needed the toilet because I almost broke down crying. This repeated itself four or five times.

As usual, people were coming into the changing room to wish Tommy luck. I felt estranged from them somehow and felt that most of them were uncomfortable with me. After all, what could any of them say to me, knowing the last time I did this, the kid I worked with died? That I had been involved in three tragedies before? Jokey, friendly Glyn was gone. Showboat? Not anymore. I felt like the grim reaper of boxing.

Finally, that knock came on the door to say it was time to go. We all hugged each other as we stood. As we walked towards the ring, my legs were shaking and when we climbed between the ropes, I looked down at Glenn McCrory, who was commentating again. It was awkward for both of us. We just nodded our heads.

Once the bell rang, I felt a little better. The immediacy of the action and all the adrenaline and cortisone of a boxing match kicked in. Tommy put on a great display of hitting and moving, to win the title over ten rounds from Doncaster's Craig Derbyshire. At the final bell, I jumped in the ring, aware that my eyes were full of tears. I didn't know if they were tears of joy or sadness. It was impossible to tell.

The emcee announced the result, then Dennis Hobson took the microphone to announce that a raffle that had taken place earlier in the evening had raised over £1,000 for Scott's girlfriend. Everyone clapped, but then Dennis unexpectedly handed me the microphone to say a few words. That totally threw me.

I got as far as thanking everyone for coming, before I broke down crying, standing in a boxing ring in front of hundreds of people. Tommy came over and hugged me. The microphone was taken off me. That was the end of my speech.

Back in the dressing room, there was of course jubilation at Tommy's first major title win, but I couldn't join in and felt guilty. It didn't seem right that people were happy and jumping around so soon after Scott had died. I sat by myself in a corner, and as I had done so much since Scott's death, I tried to get my head together.

35

I STARTED having occasional meetings with Scott's girlfriend Natalie, just to chat and to see how she was getting along. Obviously, this time was tough for her in all sorts of ways, but if nothing else, we wanted to try to help her out financially. We agreed to let things settle for a bit, then SBC would do an afternoon called the Scott Westgarth fun-day, with bouncy castles, a bucking bronco and all that stuff, to try to raise Natalie some money. She and Scott had just bought a house together and of course, like all young people, he hadn't taken out life insurance.

Scott's funeral took place on 29 May at Grenoside crematorium. Predictably, it was a very well attended and emotional affair. I read a short poem written by Andy Manning, an ex-pro who worked with me at SBC, but choked up before I got to the end and couldn't quite finish.

I felt a little better after the funeral and hoped it meant I was beginning to deal with it all. Maybe that had given me some closure? A week after the funeral, we held our fun-day. It was humbling to see how many people turned out to help and we raised a worthwhile sum for Scott's girlfriend.

As time went by, though, I had to accept that I was continuing to struggle. The scene from the ambulance would not leave my head. I kept thinking of Watson, Stone, Wilson and especially the trip in the ambulance with Sam Sheedy just before Scott's death. What the hell was that? Some kind of practice? Were all these events in my boxing life warnings? Was God or the universe trying to tell me something?

I questioned myself often, mostly about what the hell I was doing in the boxing game. What sort of a way to earn a living is this? It's a sport that demands such devotion and commitment but what does it give you, really? Is it worth it? How can it be? All my life I felt like I had just fallen into the sport, and was waiting for something else to come along, but it never had.

I was handed a distraction from my inner dialogue, when I got a call from someone at Sky TV, asking if I had heard anything about Brendan Ingle. I hadn't but rang around and it emerged that Brendan was in hospital. He was very gravely ill and sure enough, later that day, he died.

By this time, the Ingle gym had become world famous, and Brendan was widely regarded as one of the top trainers from the British Isles in the post-war era. He had almost reached iconic status. That meant his death was a major, national news story and I began receiving calls and messages from every media outlet under the sun, asking me for a reaction.

I texted Brendan's son, Dominic, to say how sorry I was, spoke to a few other people and conversations soon turned to the service. It was scheduled for the cathedral in the town centre and I knew, because of Brendan's stature in Sheffield and British boxing that it would be a huge affair, like a state funeral.

The whole thing soon turned into another messy situation. A young lady who trained at my gym worked at the cathedral and was in charge of the guest list for the funeral. One day she asked why my name wasn't on it. I was shocked to hear this and told her I honestly had no clue, because I definitely wanted to attend and pay my respects.

What made the situation odd, was that I was getting phone calls every minute about Brendan. I went on local radio, *Look North* and Calendar TV. I even appeared on Steve Bunce's show on the digital TV channel BoxNation, to speak about how Brendan had been such a massive influence in my life. I felt that I told the truth about things and that even though Brendan and I didn't always get along, there was no doubting his importance in my life.

I made arrangements to go to the funeral anyway, even if I didn't have a seat and had to stand at the back. Brendan had been too big a figure in my early years to think of missing the service.

The night before the funeral, my girlfriend booked tickets to the theatre, which was a new experience for me, to see the stage version of *One Flew Over the Cuckoo's Nest*. In the interval, I checked my phone and had received a text that really took me aback.

'Glyn – my Mom doesn't want you at Brendan's funeral tomorrow, so I hope you can respect her wishes. Tara.'

Tara was Brendan's youngest daughter, and I must admit I was shocked. I had been enjoying the play. Doing something different had helped to take my mind off all the horror of the previous couple of months, but that message immediately darkened my mood. I thought I should reply, so texted back.

'I'm so, so sorry to hear that. I so wanted to pay my respects to ur Dad but I won't go if this is your Mom's wishes. Thoughts are with you all.'

I found myself distracted for the rest of the play and when it finished, and we walked out of the Crucible Theatre, I started ranting at my girlfriend about it. It genuinely upset me that I was not allowed to attend the funeral of a man who had been a father figure to me. It didn't seem fair.

I later found out that Herol Graham and Naseem Hamed, two of Brendan's best-known fighters, were not going to be at the funeral either. I found that attitude strange, and can't claim to understand it, but the decision of the family was the decision of the family. At least the whole episode showed me how important it was that I went back to St Thomas' that day to thank Brendan in person. I will always be grateful to him and I'm happy that I managed to tell him that before he died.

After the funeral, things continued as normally as possible at Sheffield Boxing Centre. I still did not really feel myself but battled on and did my best to hide my struggles. We took some kids on a trip out to California and I continued working with Tommy Frank, my new prospect Keanen Wainwright who had just turned pro, and all the other lads in the gym.

In September, the police turned up to interview me about the events leading up to Scott's death. I was assured that this was just a routine procedure for the coroner's report, but still found it stressful. My previous dealings with police had always been quite adversarial and I had to be reassured by them that I didn't need a solicitor present. Just knowing I had to talk to them put me on edge.

That wasn't helped when an officer arrived and told me she was a murder detective. It was said casually. Nonetheless, the word murder gave me a jolt. She explained she had been a policewoman for 17 years but was ready to quit as it was starting to get to her. She told me she was sick of seeing dead bodies. I could fully sympathise with that.

We went through all the details of the days leading up to and immediately after Scott's death. There were times I felt uncomfortable with some of her questions, and moments when I felt myself getting upset. The interview lasted for two hours and when it finished, she explained that I would have to appear at Doncaster Coroner's Court to answer any questions the coroner might have. As she left, my mood was bleak. I was not looking forward to that.

At the end of October, I travelled down to London for the British Boxing Board of Control annual awards dinner at the Royal Lancaster Hotel. Robert Smith, the general secretary of the BBBoC had rung me, to ask if I thought John Westgarth would be interested in coming too. As a result, John and his partner Julie arranged to come down with me and my girlfriend, and we all booked into the same hotel.

The night was a wonderful event as usual. I always enjoyed seeing so many faces from the boxing world in one place. Robert Smith stood to give a speech about the state of British boxing and mentioned Scott Westgarth, which triggered some negative emotions. I looked sideways at John and could tell he was distressed by it too.

Various awards were handed out that night and then Robert Smith returned to the microphone to present the Henry Cooper Trophy for services to boxing. There was some preamble, as there always is with these things. I was only half listening in truth, until Smith announced, 'And the award for services to boxing 2018 goes to Glyn Rhodes, MBE.'

It was a complete shock and my heart pounded as I walked towards the stage. There had been no warning and I was unprepared, so made a dog's dinner of a speech, but everyone clapped which was very kind of them.

We stayed up until the early hours of the morning talking and celebrating, and I had a great night with John Westgarth. I never said it out loud, but I did wonder if I only got the award because of what had happened to Scott.

As usual, I couldn't sleep, so we got up early, went for breakfast and wandered around like tourists. We had a lovely day in London but as I always seem to do, I kept asking myself how we had got here and what it's all about. Everything always came back to boxing, how it made me and how it was breaking me. It seemed like you couldn't have one without the other.

One thing followed the other from there. Tommy Frank became Commonwealth super-flyweight champion, which was a fantastic evening. John Westgarth became a regular at Tommy's fights, often coming into the dressing room to offer encouragement, which was nice. Then, at one show at the Ponds Forge Arena, the doctor who had attended Scott in the ambulance after his last fight was present.

We both looked at each other and smiled as he came into the dressing room to examine the boxers. It was so strange because not one person in that room knew the connection between us and the journey from hell we made together in that ambulance.

Eventually he walked over to me, shook my hand and asked if we could have a word outside.

We went to stand out in the corridor, and he asked how I was doing. I told him how much I had struggled, but that I was getting there slowly. We kept being interrupted by passers-by, so I asked the security if we could open the fire doors as we needed a place to talk in private.

The doctor asked me what it was like for me directly after the fight and how I was feeling in my head. He also told me he had made a statement, but neither the police nor coroner had been in touch with him, which I found odd as he was the one who dealt with Scott the whole time after he left the arena. I then asked him his personal opinion of what he thought had happened, which he explained in layman's terms. In one way, that made me feel better. At least I could comprehend why Scott's body did the things it did.

By early 2019, Abbie, the wife of one of my SBC boxers, Shawn Malcolm, had planned a walk around Dam Flask, a place in the countryside where Scott Westgarth used to go running. The idea was it would mark the first anniversary of Scott's death and give us a day to commemorate him together. At the back of my mind, I still knew that I would need to appear at the coroner's court, but the date had still not been fixed.

Abbie had made a wreath which we were going to place in a particular spot with a view, which Scott always used to like. I thought this was a lovely thing to do, but had to admit that as the anniversary approached, I was not feeling good internally. The bad memories, all the fucking feathers, plagued me constantly and to make it worse, I wasn't sure what to make of news I heard regarding Scott's family. It seemed they were looking for someone to blame and possibly even sue for what had happened. They were hoping to use the coroner's case for this purpose. My solicitor told me I didn't have anything to worry about, but that didn't make me feel any better.

On the day of the walk, I headed up there with Matt Mowatt, to find that tons of people had turned up. As we parked and walked towards the crowds, I found myself getting emotional all over again. Abbie had done a great job of organising everyone and we walked the same way Scott used to run when he was training for fights. There were people with dogs and prams and even Bob Westerdale, the sports editor of the local newspaper.

We walked all the way around, then people hugged and shook hands. Everyone just went on their way, but it somehow seemed a fitting tribute and I hoped it helped other people to come to terms with what had happened.

For my part, I stayed in my regular seat on the boxing merry-go-round. Training in the gym, amateur shows, pro shows. John Westgarth continued appearing at Tommy's fights, although we didn't speak much, and I wondered what was on his mind regarding the coroner's court. The whole thing really bothered me.

Early in 2019, world heavyweight champion Anthony Joshua asked to use my gym for training, which caused a lot of excitement around the place. I enjoyed having him around and found him a class act, which provided an uplift, but shortly after that, two good friends of mine both took their own lives, one after the other, which really made me think.

I had never concerned myself with mental health discussions before, but my own issues were ongoing, while two old mates committing suicide seemed like a major signpost. I began searching online and discovered that one in four men suffer from psychological or emotional problems. The more I read, the more shocked I became. It seemed it was an epidemic.

Eighty-four men commit suicide in the UK every week, while 75 per cent of all suicides are men. Something that kept coming up was that men are less likely to speak out about their feelings, which was considered to be a contributory factor. Through this, I began to take stock of everything that had happened to me.

I started having conversations with people in the gym about it and one day, was approached by a lady who trained with me. She asked if I would be willing to speak at a meeting she was hosting, to help make people aware of mental illness. I told her I was happy to help but wasn't qualified to talk on these subjects. She was very keen though and persuaded me to do it.

The meeting was in the centre of Sheffield and when I got there, I nearly crapped myself with nerves as I was due to be the first speaker. I told the audience that over the last few years people have become more aware of mental illness and figures from the boxing world like Tyson Fury, Ricky Hatton and Frank Bruno had all come out and gone public with their stories.

I spoke also about Herol as a guy who had been having a really bad time lately. He was still based at the mental hospital in London and there was no sign of when he would be discharged. I then decided to confess and said how much I'd also been struggling myself since Scott's death, how my head just didn't seem on things any longer, how I wasn't myself.

I would have days where I'd wake up and as soon as I opened my eyes, I knew if it was going to be a good day or a bad day. I couldn't sleep and when I should have been awake, all I wanted to do was go to sleep. Then at bedtime, I was wide-eyed. It was a horrible cycle that I couldn't break out of.

The speech seemed well received by the audience but more than anything, it helped cement things in my own mind. I knew I was having serious mental health problems. Somehow saying it out loud, to a room full of strangers, made it real.

36

AS THINGS rumbled on, I felt like I was living with a cloud following me around. I had some wonderful moments, and although they provided bursts of happiness, the darkness always returned.

Tommy Frank defended the Commonwealth title and picked up a WBC 'silver' belt. There are so many silly championships in boxing now and it can get confusing even for someone who has spent their life in the sport, but it meant that he was continuing to make fantastic progress. We were all so proud of him. He was named as an ambassador for the British Heart Foundation too, which made things all the more special, to think of the inspiration he could give to kids who suffered serious illness, as he had when he was little.

In September, I took a group of young boxers over to America and through luck and a bit of help from well-known broadcasters Steve Bunce and John Rawlings, I managed to score tickets for everyone to watch Tyson Fury's contest against the German, Otto Wallin, in Vegas. The kids loved the occasion and afterwards, at the airport, we even met Fury as he made his way home. He had suffered a nasty cut in the fight and needed 47 stitches.

'It's a good job we had insurance,' he told us. 'Or we would have had to pay $20,000 for the medical bills.'

He couldn't have been more charming and took plenty of time to chat to my youngsters, which I appreciated. It did occur to me that as he had just banked several million for his fight, a $20,000 medical bill wouldn't have been a massive problem for him, but I didn't say so.

I spent Christmas with my kids and had a brilliant time in Rome for New Year, as a guest of an old friend of mine called Francisco Capuano. It was a good thing I enjoyed myself there, because once we got back from Italy, I found out that the coroner's court date had been set for 20 January, in Doncaster.

I spoke to a few friends who were police officers and asked them what to expect. I was told that it was a serious thing, which troubled me. I asked if I needed legal representation and was told not but was also told that once I was called for questioning, it could be very hard. The coroner and the police would interrogate me, as would the family's solicitor.

Luckily for me, my daughter Jorja wasn't working that day and agreed to come with me. I felt I badly needed support.

I was scheduled to be called at 11am and up to that point, was basically a spectator. So, I sat in the courtroom and looked around. Scott's family were there but all sitting separately. I had heard there were rifts between them, and this seemed to confirm it. There were reporters and representatives of the BBBoC, and various other official-looking people.

The hearing began with a pathologist who spoke about a process called 'coning' which is what had happened to Scott's brain in the ambulance. As I listened to him, I thought how bad it must be for Scott's family to sit through such a level of detail.

After that, John Westgarth was called to the stand and told the court what he observed in the changing room but said he hadn't been overly concerned. After all, Scott had just done ten hard rounds. John had been a decent pro himself and knew what he was talking about.

Next up was Natalie, Scott's girlfriend, who said she knew something wasn't right with Scott when she climbed into the ring at the end of the fight. But like his dad, she just felt it was fatigue after a hard contest.

When Natalie had finished speaking, Stefy Bull was called. Stefy had been the promoter of the show that fateful night. The court's treatment of Stefy really shocked me. They seemed to ask questions designed to catch him out, and the solicitors and the judge made him look terrible. At one point, the judge said that Stefy, as the promoter of the show, should have had a direct line to the hospital. Stefy said, well I had my phone on me at all times, to which the judge raised his eyebrows and gave a piercing look.

They asked Stefy what he was doing when Scott was being taken away to the ambulance, to which Stefy replied that he had been in the changing rooms, getting Curtis Woodhouse ready for the next fight.

'So, you, as the promotor of the show, have an injured boxer being taken to hospital and you're in the changing rooms getting the next fighter ready? Is that correct?' the solicitor asked.

Stefy didn't know what to say. I felt so sorry for him. He had done nothing that promoters of boxing shows don't do every week up and down the country, but it felt like they were trying to apportion blame for Scott's death to him.

As I waited for my turn, my left leg shook uncontrollably. What if they treated me like this? Jorja got hold of my hand and squeezed it very tight.

It was such a stressful experience as I knew the people in this room were looking for answers. No matter how many times I told myself that Scott's death wasn't my fault, I was worried that I would fuck things up and say the wrong thing, just like Stefy had. Then someone in that court would start asking me questions I couldn't answer and leave me standing there like I had blood on my hands. I felt like getting up and running out, but then, it was my turn.

So, I walked shakily to the front of the court and stepped into the witness box. As I went, I made a silent promise to myself that I wouldn't cry or get upset. That didn't last long.

I was asked to talk through the events from start to finish and began confidently enough, but, once I got to the end of the fight and the ambulance journey, I started to crack. I turned my body, so the majority of the audience couldn't see me crying and my words came out in little bursts, punctuated by sobs.

I felt naked standing there in front of those people like that. Naked and wretched and pathetic. It was another low point, in a time when I had been having so many of them.

At one point, the judge asked if I would like to sit down, to which I answered, 'Yes.' The judge then announced that there was to be a short break. I was taken into a small room along with Jorja and was shaking so badly that I couldn't stop, so I made a joke out of it and started laughing. Bravado kicked in and I stood up and started shadow boxing.

We were interrupted by a knock on the door. A lady poked her head into the room and asked if I would feel up to speaking to Becky, Scott's mum, before the case resumed.

I really wasn't sure if this was a good idea but agreed, as I could see Becky waiting behind the clerk. It was a good thing I did. She came in, put her arms round me and gave me a huge hug. That gesture made me feel so much better, as if maybe this wasn't me against them, after all.

When we returned to the courtroom and I took the stand again, I was asked why I was the one who got in the ambulance with Scott. I was also asked if I knew why the ambulance stopped en route to the hospital.

The tears came again as I answered these questions to the best of my ability. I relayed all the details of what had happened on that ambulance journey, which was the first time I had spoken about it. By the time I got to the end, I was a wreck again, but at least they told me I was free to leave.

When we got outside, Jorja threw her arms around me. I needed that. God, I was so happy she was there.

We didn't talk much on the way back from Doncaster in the car because I was going through it all in my head over and over. It had been two years since Scott's death, but it still felt so recent. The tragedy had dominated my entire life ever since it happened. I told myself it was over for me now. All I wanted was to remember Scott Westgarth as the funny, dry kid he was.

Ultimately, the court's verdict was death by brain injury, caused by misadventure. The judge even recorded in the verdict what a great fight it had been and how well Scott had done. I don't know if that's the conclusion the family were hoping for, but it seemed appropriate to me, and a fitting way to sum up the end of Scott's boxing career, and his life.

37

I WOULD like to say that was the end of the darkness, but it wouldn't be true. Despite the relief of getting the inquest out of the way, the memories of Scott's final moments stayed with me, especially at night.

That brings us back to where this book began, because after speaking to Matt Mowatt, who confessed his own sessions with a psychiatrist, I recognised that I was never going to beat this thing on my own. I needed help. That wasn't an easy thing for a guy like me to say, but I had to admit it.

I needed help.

The depth of the mental health crisis among men become increasingly clear, especially among those who are considered tough.

There were suicides among people I knew. I lost old friends. I hadn't thought any of them were struggling. While this book was being written, someone else I knew lay down in front of an oncoming train. No one knew it had been so bad for him.

Over time I became used to visiting the shrink. I even stopped storming out when I got upset. It took me a while, but I got there. I explained how Scott's death, and what his body did in that ambulance, kept coming back at me. Every time I saw an ambulance on the road, every time I took a boxer to a fight. I just couldn't stop the events of that evening from returning and overwhelming me.

'You've been hiding,' she told me. 'You've been pushing away the trauma you suffered that night. If you're ever going to move past it, you have to confront it.'

'Okay.'

'It's like a ball in a swimming pool,' she went on. 'You can push it under the water as many times as you like, but it will keep popping back up again, so you have to reach a place where you're comfortable with the ball being there.'

In her gentle, professional way, she made me talk about it again and again and again. Every session, at some point, she would look me in the eye and say, 'So, tell me.' And I would have to go through the whole story from start to finish.

At first this frustrated me, but by the end, I understood. She wanted me to get to the point where I could talk about what happened without falling to pieces. Once I got there, it would mean I was beginning to deal with it.

This way of coping also made me reflect on other things, especially the other boxing tragedies I had witnessed and the negativity and spite around my relationship with Brendan. Maybe it's natural to do that anyway as you get older?

I saw and acknowledged that boxing had done me harm in lots of ways. It's okay to say that because boxing can be a harmful thing. Anyone that denies that just isn't dealing with reality. What's hard to acknowledge, for people in and around the sport, is that you can't change or dilute that harm, because it's built into boxing and the culture which surrounds it. Boxing people can be great people, but they're not the same as folk who work in other fields. Turning up to a gym and getting punched in the face every day changes the way you see the world. It changes your relationship with violence.

Importantly though, once I finished my course of therapy and moved on, once I got to the point that Scott's death didn't consume my whole mind, I was also able to remember all the light, too. That boxing yin yang returned to full effect.

My gym was buzzing. I cannot say how proud I am of that place. Keanen 'the wolf' Wainwright was developing into a great little fighter, just like Tommy Frank. Both of them have exciting futures. Our team atmosphere was second to none, and I mean that. A lot of people describe a workplace as being like a family, but in our case, it's true. Guys like Matt Mowatt and Andy Manning gave SBC such a brotherly feel. Sam Sheedy's in there nearly every day. He's interested in taking the place over when I retire.

Meanwhile, SBC, as it has always done, continues to attract kids from some of Sheffield's most deprived areas, giving them a place to be, something to do and something to believe in. You can't put a value on that.

So, after nearly 50 years in the fight game, spent inside and outside the ropes, I find myself seeing it from both sides.

Some people want to condemn boxing. And I get that. Others want to glorify it, which I can understand, too.

Me? I don't do either. I accept the lot. Because you can't make boxing safe without destroying what makes it special. It's not part of regular society, so people who only live in that world don't understand it. But those who have laced on a pair of gloves, even if only for a spar, they know.

Boxing just is.

It exists in a place beyond good and evil.